# ONE-MINUTE SUPER DAD

Dr Prashant Jindal is an internationally renowned refractive eye surgeon, whose patients include numerous peak performance athletes, Olympic medalists and celebrities from around the world.

He is a sought-after speaker, has appeared on various talk shows and been widely interviewed on ophthalmology, parenting and health issues.

Praise for *One-Minute Super Dad*

'If every parent can read this book, the world will be a different place.'

– James Michael Lafferty, former CEO of Coca-Cola and Procter & Gamble

'Follow the advice in this book and your kids will remember the special moments with their superhero dad for the rest of their lives.'

– Stephanie Hale, author of *Millionaire Women, Millionaire You*

'Every dad owes it to his child to buy this breakthrough work.'

– Craig Richards, senior mentor, the Anthony Robbins Companies

'A triumphant must-read book and salvation to all fathers who love their families.'

– Vincent Wong, CEO, Wealth Dragons

# ONE-MINUTE SUPER DAD

## 99 Magic Moments to Raise Amazing Children

Dr Prashant Jindal

HarperCollins *Publishers* India

First published in India by
HarperCollins *Publishers* in 2018

HarperCollins Publishers India, Cyber City, Building 10-A, Gurugram, Haryana-122002, India

www.harpercollins.co.in

2 4 6 8 10 9 7 5 3 1



P-ISBN: 978-93-5277-453-1
E-ISBN: 978-93-5277-454-8



Typeset in 12/15 Century Schoolbook at
Manipal Digital Systems, Manipal

Printed and bound at
MicroPrints India, New Delhi

This product is made of FSC®-certified and other controlled material.

HarperCollins Publishers, Macken House, 39/40 Mayor Street Upper, Dublin 1, D01 C9W8, Ireland

*This book is dedicated to*
*my father, a true Super Dad*

# Contents

# Foreword

If you are like many dads, particularly the time-pressed ones, you often wonder if you are doing everything you can to help your child grow up to live to his/her full potential.

While there are plenty of books for the moms, there isn't even one great book specifically for the dads. Effective parenting has been even more difficult for the dads because there is little information available to help a dad be the best dad that he can be. Until now!

You now have a book in your hands that can transform the impact you can have on your child's life. Like most of the dads who have read this book, you will breathe a sigh of relief as you learn what you are doing right and how to tweak what is not being done in the ideal way.

I have been deeply moved by this book and know that you will be, too. Its lessons are timeless and its advice is built to last. I believe this treasury of practical, easy-to-implement ideas will fast become a classic every dad will want to own.

This book can be read in less than two hours. I believe reading and applying it will be one of the best investments you could make for the future of your child. I encourage you to tell other dads about it. I know they will thank you.

*One-Minute Super Dad* is based on extensive research conducted by the author, a physician dedicated to the well-being of others. A caring dad himself, Prashant's passion for helping others is evident here. As you begin to apply the simple breakthrough ideas in this book, you will become as passionate about it as I am.

Here's to more effective fathering for all of us! What could be more important than that? For us, for our kids, and the world they can impact in so many positive ways?

**Raymond Aaron**
Co-author of the *New York Times* best-seller
*Chicken Soup for the Parent's Soul*

# 1
# Why Is a Super Dad So Crucial Today?

A super dad is a father who is able to raise his child to be a stable, healthy, confident individual, composed in all situations, and one who responds rather than reacts to situations and problems that life throws at him when he grows up.

Every father, despite the tough grind of life, does the absolute best in his remit to give the best to his child. For most men, the years between thirty and forty-five are both the most crucial and the most productive years of their careers. Men cannot compromise much with their careers during this period. I was no exception either. So, instead of being frustrated at times, which I very often was, I had to find ways to parent my children even when I was most hard-pressed for time.

I just have one humble request to you – now that you have picked up this book, *please have an open mind* to all the things talked about here. By the time you get to the end of the book, you will see that it all starts making sense.

The importance of parenting is borne by the fact that how we treat our children in the first ten to twelve years determines or shapes the course of their entire lives.

I am a surgeon by profession, not a psychologist or counsellor. In my journey as a parent, I have been through numerous successes. *One-Minute Super Dad* is a part of my mission to help fathers around the world, especially the busy ones, in giving their very best to their kids with whatever time and resources they have. The time spent on commute and travel in India has significantly increased for all of us, not to mention the increased stress and insecurities, leaving most fathers with just a handful of minutes to spend with their kids each day. This book addresses how to use those few minutes to great effect to keep children inspired.

Success leaves clues. To bring up my two children well, I needed the experience of parents who had older children and I also needed to learn from their mistakes and achievements. To be very sure about getting the right information and not just depending on hearsay, I reached out to hundreds of parents from all walks of life, including top psychiatrists, authors, counsellors and experts on child behaviour. I even tracked down the parents of people I looked up to and adored, and requested them to share the secrets of their success in matters of parenting.

Please allow me to share some facts and figures I discovered in my research during my journey that left me frightened. This data also highlights the fact that effective and supportive parenting is very crucial today, like never before, especially for parents in India.

- Ten per cent of five- to fifteen-year-olds have a diagnosable mental health disorder in India. 'Family dynamics plays a vital role in mental health and illness and child rearing practices significantly affect the child's development ...' Indian Journal of Psychiatry, 2010.
- A study shows that 15 per cent of adolescents in Delhi thought of suicide and 5 per cent actually attempted it (Dr Sharma et al.).
- Ninety per cent of alcohol consumed by underage drinkers is during binge drinking.
- The rate of obesity in six- to eleven-year-olds is an average 19.6 per cent, and in under-fives, 12.4 per cent. The percentage has tripled in the last thirty years.
- Suicide rates in India are highest in the 15– age group.
- Eight per cent of the adult population has diabetes. Ninety per cent of individuals having Type 2 diabetes are obese.
- Six per cent of parents seek medical help for their children for difficulties with emotion, concentration or behaviour.

- About 25 per cent of parents in developing countries are single. Kids of single parents are three times more likely to need psychological help.
- Out of all children's hospital admissions 10.5 per cent are due to mental health problems.
- Of all school-age children 3–5 per cent of have ADHD (Attention Deficit Hyperactivity Disorder) and the treatment is based on strong drugs like amphetamines, despite evidence that behavioural therapy is highly effective.

Don't the above-mentioned facts and figures prompt us into realizing that it is time we act and change our kids' mindsets? We can hugely reduce the chances of our kids going through these devastating, depressing and deplorable problems by doing and saying certain things consistently.

Attempting to address all the problems at one go would be overwhelming, but by taking a step-by-step and minute-by-minute approach, child rearing can be made easier and may prove unbelievably rewarding. I refer to the Japanese philosophy of Kaizen – 'Constant improvement by taking small steps'.

*One-Minute Super Dad* is full of valuable snippets that make the big picture look better. I have introduced the concept of 'One-Minute Magic' – these are things that can be said or done in just a minute but leave a huge, positive and long-lasting impact. Additionally, there are 'One-Minute Grenades' – these are bad habits that are to be nipped. Just one minute is all you need to make a difference, provided it is done consistently.

*One-Minute Super Dad* is meant specifically for dads with kids ranging from newborns and toddlers to twelve-year-olds, though many parents with teenaged children gave the feedback that they too found it helpful. In the first decade of the lives of our kids, subconscious software, which will run a lifetime, is being written on their tender hearts and minds. If this subconscious software is coded correctly, it will drive them to achieve great things. Small mistakes will leave bugs in their systems, which may cause future challenges. By the time a child is ten, his entire personality has already been formed. His language, thinking and habits are well ingrained in him.

Let us look at the good things that we can control and make them happen. The destiny of our kids is in our hands. Every child has within him seeds of greatness. All we have to do is to provide the right environment to nurture them. We do not have to reinvent anything.

It might take some time, perseverance and repetition, but eventually children adopt the right habits and thoughts that will form the foundations for the rest of their lives.

Kids will want to cooperate if we make them believe that we are on their side. Often, kids do not need a solution. They just need to be listened to.

*One-Minute Super Dad* is the briefest possible summary of the answers I found to my questions, especially for Indian parents who have an extremely busy life, whose kids are growing up in an extremely competitive environment. I hope you enjoy reading the book and never ever forget that childhood is the most beautiful of life's seasons.

Having studied every possible aspect of childhood problems, in summary, there are three pillars of parenting:

- Communication
- Role modelling
- Quality time

These three headings also form the backbone of *One-Minute Super Dad*. The remaining chapters address how we can make fathering a more joyous and fun-filled experience.

Shiv Khera famously said, 'Winners do not do different things; they do things differently.' Napoleon Hill, author of one of the most respected classics to date, *Think and Grow Rich*, said, 'A person has absolute control over none but one thing on this earth ... and that is what goes into his mind.' This is a crucial lesson for every parent, as it is our responsibility to make sure that the right stuff finds its way into the minds of our children. If we can get positive and valuable learning imbibed in our children in the early years of their lives, it will stay with them for their entire lifetime and they can take better and more informed decisions rather than merely conform.

The 'One-Minute Magics' will help you realize that you can make a huge difference in shaping your kid's life in just sixty seconds on many occasions. The book is based on knowledge and experience gained both from people in India and from many living abroad for, universally, every parent across the world wishes for his child to be happy no matter where he lives. You, my reader, may find that some points in this book do not find to apply to your particular situation while some others that may only partially apply. However, the vast majority of tips outlined here would work for everyone.

India is increasingly on the move, and we are shorter of time today than ever before. Travelling by the metro, playing by the odd–even traffic rules, frequent Indian political changes do not help matters. But we can still make the most of whatever family time we have. Hopefully, this book will show you how to do just that. In many instances, one minute is all you really need. Turn to the pages here when you feel overwhelmed, frustrated, or simply at a loss. And here you will find practical solutions that take only one minute to apply.

In sixty seconds (practised consistently over a period of time), we can help our children either soar high, reach for the stars and realize their dreams or we can put them down, leaving them feeling utterly hopeless and worthless. The choice is ours.

Let me explain the two phrases I mentioned earlier, which I have used throughout the book.

**One-Minute Magic**: Positive reinforcements that help children feel great about themselves and subconsciously move them towards great things by cultivating good habits and beliefs.

**One-Minute Grenade**: Words, expressions, actions and put-downs that are capable of destroying a child's self-confidence and immensely impacting him/her negatively.

The disturbing truth is that most kids get an average of five to ten focussed minutes a day from their dads – these are those few empty minutes when they are not typing a text or responding to an email, or thinking of something else.

The purpose of *One-Minute Super Dad* is to focus on the things that can be said, done or demonstrated in the smallest amount of time. Guys, gear up, no more excuses!

This book is designed to be a read of less than a couple of hours, with certain topics deliberately repeated at different places in the book. There is a reason behind this, to let the points register better and for purposes of reiteration. It is an extremely easy, informal and fun read, hardly a typical To-Do book, and the feedback I received from the people who read my manuscript was so tremendous that whilst editing it, I only made it even simpler and more bindaas. The idea is that any father with any level of education and sophistication can read this and put it to use in some way or the other and get guaranteed results.

Also, there will be some suggestions/points that you feel are not for you for some reason or the other. Move on from those and extract from the ones that appeal to you and seem more easily doable in your circumstances.

Admittedly, anything worthwhile in life is achieved over a period of time. A doctor, an artist, executive, or athlete is good at what he does because he has dedicated hours, years and probably decades in becoming the best in his chosen field. Good fathering is no exception either. Every dad needs some of these rituals to be a 'good dad'. Anybody who has achieved greatness has got it by practising certain rituals over and over again. Life is all about striving to improve and making ourselves better than before.

When you have finished reading the book, please write down the areas you want to turn around. As a One-Minute Super Dad, create your own individual mission statement and then take action. Writing things down is always a better way of making things happen. Things will start taking shape and will look far simpler than they once did. All it takes is a minute and no more.

# 2

# Laying the Foundation: The First Twelve Years

## The Story of a Typical New Dad

Here's what a new dad typically goes through, emotionally. The nine-month-long wait ends and the baby arrives. The first-time dad holds it in his trembling arms with much excitement and curiosity, eager to see that its limbs are perfect. He touches the child gingerly with love and felicity. And just as the baby starts crying or squealing, the dad is clueless as to how to handle this bundle of joy. He's a bit scared too.

I remember when my wife was pregnant; it all seemed so easy, the idea of being a dad. No worries, no tensions. All I had to do was to follow the doctor's appointments, exclaim oohs and aahs over the ultrasound images and come back home feeling happy that our baby was growing well inside the womb. Easy.

But now I have a squealing baby who is thrashing out her arms in all directions and neither does she herself know what she wants nor I can make out anything! Her mom too is feeling fragile and uncomfortable. How do I do the right thing and take care of my wife and also help my baby blossom outside the haven of her mother's womb?

The doctor said the hormonal stuff will go away and my wife will recover soon, but what about our newborn? How do I make her life enjoyable, happy and stress-free? That was my constant thought.

Almost every father knows and understands all the scientific details, but what he doesn't realize is that *parenting is an art, not a science.*

Holding his child for the first time gives a man a new perspective of life. The precious little soul depends on him for its survival, guidance, security and love. In India, we have the highest prevalence of joint families but the greatest impact on the children's minds still comes from the parents. Both science and yoga affirm the fact that there are a lot of things said and done in life which, though not consciously remembered, are recorded in our subconscious mind which forms our beliefs and patterns of thought. This is most active in the first few years of life, when the baby is like a sponge absorbing water.

### The Subconscious Mind and Its Importance

The word 'subconscious' appears throughout this book, highlighting how powerful and influential our brains actually are.

The dictionary definition of *subconscious* is:

*adjective*
Existing or operating in the mind beneath or beyond consciousness: the subconscious self

*noun*

1. The totality of the mental process of which the individual is not aware
2. Unmeasurable mental activities

More than 80 per cent of what we do or say and how we behave is a result of our subconscious programming rather than our conscious choices. Any sports or business coach will tell you his job is 80 per cent about changing his trainee's subconscious belief system. The mechanics, muscles and tricks make up just 20 per cent of the game.

An infant's brain has no cognitive ability to resolve fear and trauma. Instead, the information it receives goes into its subconscious mind. This happens till the age of nine or ten when the brain keeps taking in huge amount of information and stores it for the future use.

One of the most effective ways of developing a positive frame of mind and thought pattern in the child is encouraging child constantly and repeatedly.

### The Importance of Encouragement

Encouragement is a cornerstone of a child's development. Dr Sugata Mitra, professor of educational technology at the school of education, communication and Language Sciences at Newcastle University, England, has proved this with an experiment he did over many years in which illiterate kids (not even knowing English) were left to handle computers. They did not have any teachers to teach them. After some time, not only did the kids figure out English but they also figured out how to use the computers, and even learnt about things like the replication of DNA and connections of neurons. So immense is the power of encouragement that children can figure out virtually anything.

Encouragement is the most important tool in the parenting toolbox. Indian children grow in an extremely competitive school environment and need a lot of confidence in their ability to think independently and solve complex problems and situations. All too often, they do have the technical ability and skills as they grow but lack the confidence that they can perform to a very high level and handle tough situations.

Problem-solving skills can be developed by the smallest tasks in the house. Discussing issues that need some input from family members or asking how the child handled a problem in school gives him confidence in his abilities and reinforces self-belief that builds over time.

The child needs to eventually grow up to be an independent individual who can take decisions without flinching and can think out of the box when the situation demands it. He must be resilient, when faced with adversities – emotional, financial and others. He must feel confident and capable when faced with challenges from his colleagues and superiors, his family, his clients and more.

As Indians, we are all very quick to criticize children at the slightest lack of performance or results, especially academic ones, and that is often the nidus for a lot of problems, including sibling rivalry. A medical entrance exam in India has about two lakh students competing for about two thousand seats – that's about one in hundred. Similar figures exist for engineering and other branches of study. To go out there and win a place needs immense self-belief and confidence, which is something that cannot be given to the person a few weeks or months before such events, but is a belief inculcated very early on in his life.

# 3
# Communication and Perception

The art of communication is based on understanding that nothing should be assumed. Individual perception shapes reality for a person and it could well be totally different from the actual reality visible to others.

Effective communication is vital, not just to be able to convey but also to ensure that what is conveyed is understood, digested and followed. The first half of this chapter summarizes the importance of this and the second half outlines some applications of this concept.

We communicate with our children by the things we say, and even more with the things we do not say. ‘Over 90 per cent of communication is non-verbal,’ based on research by Fromkin & Rodman published in the book *An Introduction to Language*. Whether we realize it or not, both the verbal and the non-verbal communication we have with our children, whether negative or positive, will shape their thinking and behaviour. It is paramount to establish good communication patterns with them. The earlier, the better.

Kids in India get a lot of homework from school and often need parents’ help with it – this is a golden time when a lot of things can be subtly communicated along with the subject. Also, the way we handle their mistakes and comment on them hugely affects their confidence. When we say, this is so because I am telling you so, it completely shuts the kids’ minds to learning positively. Even if criticism is needed, it can be really constructive.

Quality answers and solutions come from the art of asking quality questions. And if you take time asking questions, make sure you allow enough time for answers as well.

 **1. One-Minute Magic**

Ask these questions:

- What was the best part of your day?
- What was the funniest thing that happened today?
- What did you learn?
- What did you learn from (name an activity or an experience)?
- Was it difficult or easy for you?
- Will you do anything differently in the future based on what you learned today?
- Ask them to complete the sentence: 'In the future I will ...'

Some of your greatest teaching opportunities will be unplanned. So, stay alert for those opportunities in your everyday living.

**Power of the Brain**

We see with our brains and not with our eyes. Eyes only refract the light. How can we change our perception of our children if we see them incorrectly?

Now, how do you see your children? Do you see them as lovable and capable little humans, full of potential? Or do you see them as unruly, rude, lazy and shy? Our children may well become the way we see them. They will pick up on your verbal and non-verbal communication, which is hugely influenced by our perception of them. Here's how:

### Rosenthal Experiment (shocking proof)

In 1963, Robert Rosenthal wanted to prove the effects of seeing with our brains through an experiment he conducted. He told a teacher that he had a new way of testing children to see if they 'had it', referring to the traits associated with leadership and success. After his testing, he presented his findings by telling the teacher about which students had scored the highest for 'having it in them' and which ones had scored low.

At the end of the school year, he returned to collect the teacher's data on the students. He discovered that every student he had targeted as a 'star student' got the highest test scores and were leaders in the class. He also noted that the students who he said 'did not have it' received mediocre test scores and grades.

The experiment did not test the children at all. It was just for show and the man had just randomly given 'star' names to the teacher. It was the teacher who was being tested. Because the teacher believed the selected students were the leaders, they actually became leaders. The ones branded mediocre became just that. An experiment like this would never be permitted today, and rightly so. The potential for harm to the children in the experiment would negate the value of the entire exercise and it should never have been allowed.

Even so, this questionable experiment is a proof of how powerfully our perception of our children affects them. Even more importantly, it shows that all this can be deeply influenced by external factors.

## Visualization

Another principle governing the power of our brains is visualization. All action entails visualization; to put it simply, whatever is created in material is first created in the mind. An example is an experiment on basketball players split into three parts – wherein one group did only visual rehearsals of imagining that they were scoring, a second group physically practised, and the third group did not do anything for a period of four weeks. Surprisingly, the group simply visualizing were miles ahead of the one doing nothing and almost as good as the ones physically practising regularly.

Visual sight and the mind's eyes are inseparable. What we see with our eyes is a combination of reality and our perceptions. Often, people see what they want to see and miss the bigger picture as the mind is just too focussed on one thing.

Learning the power of visualization and implementing it is a great parenting tool. Experience makes us aware of the effects of our mind's eye and the world around us. For example, if we envision a task to be difficult, it will be difficult. If our perception of that task is changed, we will find the task easy. This works with our own brains as well as our children's.

If we draw images to show our children the things we want to happen, soon their perception will also change and they will take our perception to be true. It sounds very abstract, but it's actually very practical.

Here are a couple of examples to show how a One-Minute Grenade can be turned into a One-Minute Magic:

### One-Minute Grenade vs One-Minute Magic

'Is your room always so messy?'

The mental picture is of a messy room and the child will respond accordingly.

**vs**

'Your room looks so good when it is clean.'

The mental picture is of a helpful child and a clean room.

'Why are you always so wiggly?'

**vs**

'It feels so good to relax.'

### The Power of Focus

The brain works in a strange way. Wherever focus goes, energy flows. We simply attract and move towards what we are more focussed on. An analysis of highway accidents showed that when a driver lost control, he focussed on *'I must not hit the pole'*, and hence subconsciously was focussed on the pole instead of the bigger empty space. In essence, the advice is to focus on the space, i.e., on what you want and *NOT* on what you do not want.

We must be very consistent, careful and sensitive of the picture that we draw in our brains as this story proves:

A father bought a bike so that he could go riding with his children. On one particular bike ride, the father, his son and his daughter were playing 'follow the leader on their bikes'. The daughter Varsha was the leader, the son Varun was in the middle and the dad took up the rear.

The rule was that everyone not only had to follow the bike but also had to copy the actions of Varsha, the leader, for instance, zigzagging down the street. This went on for some time until Varsha turned a corner where there was a huge rose bush that she drove around. She shouted, 'Watch out for the rose bushes.'

Varun followed, calling, 'Watch out for the rose bushes.' By then, the father's focus was entirely on the rose bushes rather than the far bigger grass in the front and so he rode directly into them – much to his kids' amusement.

If the kids had said, 'Go *around* the rose bushes,' those bushes might not be the legend they are today. It is for the same reason why so many times in highway accidents, when the drivers lose control, they hit the pole as they are overtly focussed on the pole rather than the space between the poles which are a hundred metres apart!

## Communicating about Good Health and Diet to Kids

One of the biggest problems children in the developed countries (and now in the developing countries too) face is obesity. Approximately 25 per cent of children are obese, which vastly increases the likelihood that they will be obese as adults as well. Obesity can lead to very serious health problems – one of the worst is getting diabetes, a disease that is already touching epidemic levels.

As far as good health is concerned, children are too young to make decisions about what is good or bad for them. The responsibility to ensure that children are eating healthy falls squarely upon the parents. Look for opportunities to talk to your children about eating healthy foods, but be tactful, bearing in mind that children will easily turn a deaf ear to constant nagging. We need to enter their world by being very articulate in conveying our point, bearing in mind that their perception about health would become their sense of reality.

##  2. One-Minute Magic

When you serve them healthy food, say, 'Oh, this is so yummy and helps you become big and strong. These foods will help you grow.'

You can reinforce this by reminding them how it worked for other people they know. For example, you could tell them, 'Do you know why Michael Phelps won all those Olympic gold medals? One of the reasons was because he ate lots of good food. He did not eat candy that would have slowed him down. He ate lots of nutritious food that helped him build his muscles.' Finding out their worthy role models helps us get better points of leverage to mould kids.

Good eating habits at a young age are stored in the subconscious mind and lead to good choices when the kids become adults. These habits stay on for a lifetime.

In order to anchor a positive feeling with the idea of healthy food, point to a photo of your kids and say, 'You looked so handsome/pretty on that day. I guess you must have had a healthy meal.' Compliments never fail. In fact, they often produce the desired results. A pat on the shoulder has never been known to hurt anybody.

Parents' eating habits are one of the single most important influences on kids. In the early formative years, the diet has to be very high in particular nutrients like essential amino acids, minerals and vitamins. Their diet has to have a good balance of proteins, carbohydrates and fats. Most kids' diets have just too many carbohydrates which not only slows them down a lot but also causes serious health issues.

In the first decade of life, fat cells are capable of both hyperplasia (increase in the number of fat cells) and hypertrophy (increase in the size of fat cells), whereas, in adults, the fat cells can undergo hypertrophy alone. So, if the kids overeat in the early years of life without adequately burning calories, they carry an increased number of fat cells for the rest of their lives. This will make them more prone to gaining weight in adult life. This could be very frustrating and will need tremendous effort then to avoid weight gain. Such kids are also more susceptible to diabetes.

### 3. One-Minute Magic

Give your kids Vitamin D drops and omegas every morning. Vitamin D is the most common deficiency in children in India. It takes a minute, reinforces your commitment to their health and gives you an opportunity to say to them something like, 'You seem to be getting stronger bones and stronger muscles, better stamina and a healthy glow.' The list of possible things to say and the inspiration is endless. But the key is *consistency*.

##  4. One-Minute Magic

Make a list of healthy fruits and vegetables and talk about one of them every day. Select a 'vegetable or fruit of the week' and have a one-minute talk on it for one week. This educates them about diet and nutrition, which is missing in the school curriculum.

Sports and exercise too are important for kids. Computers and video games have decreased physical activity significantly. My daughter was five when she began being tutored in maths, conforming to her competitive peers. We soon decided to stop it and had her join martial arts and dance instead. Kids certainly need to be good at academics, but we need to take care of their physical and creative development too.

One of the best investments is to have a trampoline (rebounder) in the house, maybe even in the TV room. They are easily available in most sports equipment shops in India now. Kids love jumping around on it. NASA believes rebounding is the greatest exercise on earth.

If a trampoline is not available, a short dance session together with the kids can set the landscape of the house early in the morning. The spirits are lifted, the immune system is kick-started, the circulation is accelerated, the body is flushed with oxygen, and your kid's laughter will put the entire family in a better mood.

Enrol the kids in at least one form of self-defence. It is a great exercise, a confidence booster, and makes it highly unlikely that they will ever be bullied. They may, however, not want to join in the beginning. In such cases, try some one-minute silly-looking Sultan-like moves or watch some inspiring movies together, such as *Milkha Singh* or *Mary Kom*. Doing this for a few days prior to the enrolment and glorifying the skills will change your kid's perception. My four-year-old son used to cry when he joined karate. I made the mistake of not preparing him prior to his enrolment in the classes. So I withdrew him and for a couple of months, subtly made some remarks and comments about its advantages and what good it would do for him. I also found out he was obsessed with a role model who I then linked to martial arts, as his hero had a strong body. I re-enrolled him two months later and this time around, he was excited to join. He now happily does it once a week.

## Siblings

Let us give our kids the gift of the most valuable friendship for their life – their sibling. To cultivate teamwork spirit, it is important to have the kids grow like a team. Is it not strange that many siblings who were once together virtually 24/7 grow into adults who have no connection and rarely miss or think about each other, even when they have not met for years?

Although there are certainly significant other factors affecting the relationship, a slight tweak in the thought process or attitude towards each other at a young age can make a big difference.

If kids are fighting, ask them for some teamwork. When disagreement or squabbling starts, change the topic to something like 'what we are having for dinner tonight' and then go on about it. No need to make them hug each other or give lectures on friendship and sharing. It never works. Kids are very resilient and forgiving. They will be playing together soon, anyway.

## 5. One-Minute Magic

As a simple exercise, ask your children, 'What was one good thing that your brother or sister

I personally feel that kids should not have a personal smartphone. Access to mobile Internet 24/7 without any filters makes the kids vulnerable to the dangers of pornography and violence. Besides pornographic content, a lot of brutally violent videos are also viewed reguarly by children – these are videos that even most adults would find disturbing and many of these go rapidly viral in teenage circles.

Further, it's extremely important to teach kids to speak in person and over the phone, instead of communicating only through social media portals, texts or emails. Social skills are deteriorating fast and more and more children are confining themselves to the digital world rather than truly socializing. And the newspapers are full of articles about paedophiles in disguise using these platforms to lure children.

A study by Dr Sanjeev Davey shows that smartphones have immense social and psychological effects on Indian kids and are highly addictive. Whether our child is ready for a phone of their own is more a matter of preparedness than age. If you're facing this issue, here are a few questions you can ask yourself and your kid to help you determine if they are ready for a phone.

**Ask yourself:**

- Does your child need the phone to stay connected with you or for emergency situations?
- Does your child understand and respect the time and usage limits you have set down for other things like television and video games?
- Does your child understand what types of apps are okay to download and how to surf the Internet safely?
- Does your child know how to use the phone safely and appropriately? (Does he/she know whom and whom not to communicate with? What he/she should and shouldn't share online? What sorts of words and pictures *NOT* to send?

## Teaching Kids about How Others Perceive Us

We are selling ourselves at every point in our life, no matter what we do. Even as parents, we have to sell our ideas to children on a daily basis. Basic selling skills have to be taught from an early age.

## 9. One-Minute Magic

On Saturdays, give your kids the chance to make some decisions not only for themselves but also for the whole family. If the decision is unreasonable and unworkable, discuss things with them as you would with an adult, e.g., let them choose a restaurant or a movie or which clothes to wear. This will help immensely in building their confidence and make them feel important.

Ask them for their opinion on where the family could cut down on expenses (if that is an issue in the house). You will be amazed to see how brilliant and creative kids can be! I have heard from numerous parents how a comment or a suggestion of their kids has solved a complex problem at home.

## The Art of Delayed Gratification

Stressful lifestyles have led to a culture of 'I want it right now' which can be called *instant gratification*. My friend, Dr John Gray, author of *Men Are from Mars, Women are from Venus* and *Children Are from Heaven*, told me that if a parent can teach one skill to his child, it ought to be *delayed gratification*. This applies to everything in life. Kids who have learned this skill are the ones who persevere harder in life. They get stronger and subsequently work harder towards their goals and make their dreams a reality. He added that the acquired skill of delayed gratification makes children become super achievers in their personal and professional lives, besides making them learn the importance of being patient and earnest.

Children who have learned the skill of delayed gratification can bounce back in life anytime.

They are also more satisfied even when they may not have everything they want but they just do not give up.

In addition, by giving children the love and attention that they need, materialistic things become much less important for them.

We must focus on what our kids need rather than what they think they want. If we don't do this, we will have an unending list of 'I want' and a never-satisfied child.

## 10. One-Minute Magic

It is very important that we handle conflicts with love, compassion and, most importantly, consistency. If your child is pressing you for a chocolate or to watch a movie or to buy him a toy, and you have already said no, you have to stay consistent. Be firm, but do not raise your voice or give in when your child throws a tantrum. That would be seen as a weakness of yours and after some time, such tantrums would not just increase in frequency but in intensity too. Also, your consistent behaviour would teach them delayed gratification.

If the wishes of your child are reasonable and you approve of them, you can say that he or she can have it, but not now, maybe a few days later (if you so plan). It is important that your child understands that one cannot always have his way, and especially that throwing a tantrum is not acceptable and will not yield the results he is expecting. It is also important that you remember to raise the quality and not the tone or volume of your argument, if you are struggling to convince.

## Mental Toughness

A boxer was once asked how he had such strong muscles. The boxer replied, 'I get such strong muscles by subjecting them to an increased resistance every day. This is called *building by demanding*.'

Kids have to learn that challenges and problems are an integral part of our life. Letting them deal with the smallest challenges like homework issues or helping them only partly rather than spoon-feeding them helps improve their confidence and skills greatly and empowers them. It is important to identify when it is best to offer our support to them and when it is best to let them figure out a way on their own. Their creative and problem-solving muscles need to get stronger. This also helps in enhancing their cognitive and noetic abilities.

A very common problem in the 5–12 year age group is the attitude of a particular friend towards them which they find bothering them. Someone could be bullying them or causing them discomfort in some way. We must keep a close watch, but we should first advise and motivate them to solve it themselves. Too often, parents would just head straight to the class teacher or headmaster without letting kids try and solve it themselves.

## 11. One-Minute Magic

Work together on small problems in the house. For instance, we can say, 'This looks like a problem, but let us take it as a challenge and solve it.' Let the kids make suggestions. This develops and strengthens children's abilities when faced with negatives in life. For example, if they are bullied at school or not getting along well or facing hectic sports/academic/extra-curricular schedules and issues, they do not feel stressed or helpless. Instead, they learn to articulate and breeze their way through it. They have to learn how to figure a way out when the going gets tough and we, of course, are watching them from the fence and can jump in to their rescue, if required.

###  12. One-Minute Magic

Ask your children to write down the good qualities in their role models. Ask them to read it to you once a month for one minute. It tells you of their deepest feelings about what they like and appreciate. Give them full permission to change it once in a while and ask them to discuss and share their reasons for it. For example, they could stop liking a rock star after reading about his drug problems.

###  13. One-Minute Magic

Tell them about a time when you had to face a difficult issue and say, 'I got stuck with a challenge at the office today. Then I remembered how you repaired your toy the other day and it just made me feel so confident that I could solve my challenge too. It reminded me how good you are at handling your problems.' They like it when we appreciate them and they are convinced when we give proof of our appreciation. It acts like a big confidence-building injection.

###  14. One-Minute Magic

Make a one-minute video of your kids talking about a challenge they have overcome. Also, record it in their Magic Moments Diary. It will serve as a happy memory for a lifetime.

## 15. One-Minute Magic

Show your kids that their presence is helping you live a better life. Tell them, 'You know, whenever I feel a bit upset, I think of you and it brings a smile back on my face.' They will feel very proud and it will boost their self-confidence tremendously. It's a simple and obvious way but is rarely used or said. Never assume that they know it—tell it again and again.

### Relationships

When visiting one of my close friends, I noticed he had framed a photo of his wife in a heart-shaped photo frame with a bow going across it. He told me he used it to influence his kids' opinions on relationships. In fact, he was using a One-Minute Magic on a regular basis to influence his kids.

##  16. One-Minute Magic

My friend would repeatedly adore the picture in front of the kids and just say, 'Your mummy was my girlfriend and I love her so much. God has blessed me with such a lovely life partner. I am proud of her and our relationship.'

At a subconscious level, they are being subtly taught that relationships are ideally meant to be long-term.

This makes it more likely that our child will value the importance of having a stable partner and have longer-lasting and fulfilling relationships.

### Sex Education

A dad goes to his twelve-year-old son and proposes they talk about sex. The son says, 'Okay, what do you want to know, Dad?'

Jokes aside, the responsibility of sex education lies squarely on the shoulders of the parents. The national media sex education campaigns teach them how to have protected sex but place no emphasis on the damaging psychological impact teenage sex has over many kids, especially girls. As an effect, the campaigns have only increased teenage sex because, instead of teaching or advising them to restrain themselves from having sex even when they are sure of their partners, we are encouraging them to go ahead. The campaigns should place emphasis on 'prevention is better than cure'. We should begin teaching our children proper attitudes toward their own bodies when they are very young. Children are naturally curious and want to know how their bodies work. They want to know where babies come from.

If a child holds out his small cup of inquiry, we should not pour an ocean of explanation into it. At the same time, we should not shirk having a discussion on the subject. Generally, they will be content with a simple answer. Sex education can start even at the age of three. Before the age of ten, the child is learning all about it from his peers anyway. What would you prefer: them learning it in a playground where you have no control over what they are told or learning it from you?

## 17. One-Minute Magic

*Cautioning them about abuse in a subtle way:* Tell your children that smart kids know how to protect themselves and their bodies. Over 60 per cent of child abuse happens at the hands of a close relative or a known friend. Explaining this fact subtly would significantly slim down the chances of it happening to them. We need to be our kids' confidant and teach them to be smart and careful.

###  18. One-Minute Magic

*Creating awareness via a news article*: Since it is an uncomfortable topic for many Indians, if you feel that the above subtle way doesn't convey the point well, it helps to use a news item, recent or old, to convey the point and warn the child and make him aware of the possibility of such nasty incidents occuring.

###  19. One-Minute Magic

It's very important to know how special our children are to us and make them feel so by saying it and to provide regular support, encouragement and self-worth. For example, say to your daughter, 'You are a very special girl', and she will act that way. It is fascinating how the opinion of those we care about shapes the way we act. If our friends tell us we are always hungry, pretty quickly we truly are. The subconscious mind is incredibly powerful. We can use this to our children's advantage and help our children be the best by telling them they already are special and what we want them to be.

## 20. One-Minute Magic

Ask questions to stimulate participation and creativity, such as:

- Why do we need to do it this way?
- How else can we do this?

This could be homework, a problem or even craftwork.

## 21. One-Minute Magic

In order to show your kids that you are curious to know their thoughts as well as to encourage analytical thinking, seek their opinions:

- What do you think about ...?
- How do you feel about ...?
- Do you remember an experience like ...?

## 22. One-Minute Magic

Write a note for your child telling him why he is special and surprise him by slipping it under the pillow, in a lunchbox, or into his pocket. The feeling they experience when they read it is simply great to witness!

###  23. One-Minute Magic

Emotions are powerful ways to anchor an experience or a thought. To teach your kids this skill, ask questions like:

- What is your favourite ...?
- What makes you happy?
- What makes you sad?

This makes both parents and kids more aware of what is going on in their minds and brings latent feelings to the surface which we can address at an early stage rather than wait for a point when they have turned into problems.

#### Teaching Compassion

Encourage forgiveness. Life is too short to hold on to anger, sadness or hate. With love, compassion and forgiveness, we have room for growth and inner strength. Every day is a gift to be alive and grateful for.

###  24. One-Minute Magic

Put aside a few moments each day to remember what life is about and what is important. Explain that everyone makes mistakes, even superheroes and those we love the most. That it is human to be wrong at times, and that making a mistake is actually learning in disguise. Therefore, it is wise to forgive what others might call mistakes. Tell them that we are in this life to make mistakes and grow, and not to fake perfection and stumble in the shadows of our lies. Suppose we may hear, '... was mean to me today.' We can suggest, 'Let's forgive him today and give him another chance,' unless the other person has done something significant which needs addressing or has to be dealt with.

###  One-Minute Grenades

- Avoid criticism.
- Avoid giving lectures. Enter their world and be articulate instead.
- Never kill a child's idea. Ask for more details, even if you are not interested.
- Never make promises you cannot keep.
- Monitor the media. Children can easily get confused as to what is real and true and what is good or bad.
- Never, ever shout. We do not realize how much we wound and intimidate our children when we shout or raise our voice. These wounds are carried in the subconscious mind

throughout their lives. Raise the quality and not the volume of your point.

- Do not 'fear-dominate' your children. It actually creates more unruly and negative children.
- Never use your feelings of hurt or anger towards your children. Never say, 'Don't trouble me more. I am already having a tough time at the office as my boss is giving me hell.' Kids start blaming themselves for their parents' hurt, anger or disappointments without much thought.
- Never threaten your children.
- Never speak negatively to your children about anyone.
- Do not judge your children. They will start to hide their mistakes for fear of disapproval.
- Never punish them in public. Feedback should be given to them in private. Have a secret signal to use in public, indicating they need to change what they are saying or doing. They will appreciate the parent who allows them to save face.
- Minimize stress by gently explaining rather than by shouting.
- Avoid rhetorical questions. They only make the child uncooperative.

Material things can be cleaned, mended and replaced easily without any fuss, but a heart broken through harsh words or by neglect may take a lifetime to repair. As a helpful tool, get the downloadable poster from the resources section on our website to assist you with this.

Children can feel our energy and it is vital that they feel our presence too. Hug your child every day and say, 'You are my most precious thing in the world.' After all, a hug a day keeps the psychiatrist away.

# 4
# Spending Quality Time

We are normally too busy to spend regular focussed time with kids doing 'nothing'. When we are with them, we are normally checking our phone or email or solving somebody's problem.

As a One-Minute practice, get into the habit of putting aside some time every day just to talk, ask questions, interact and communicate effectively with your kids. The One-Minute method may help prevent a lifetime of remorse of not spending enough time with your children.

Let me share a short story of a boy who requests his father to take him on a fishing day trip to a local lake. They spend the entire day there with no success and not a single fish caught. The father texted his wife, saying that it was one of the most unproductive days of his life. The son told her, however, that it was one of best days of his life as he had his father just to himself for an entire day. What we remember most are not the big events of our life but the small joyous moments that we treasure. The power of these moments cannot be underestimated in the bonding between kids and parents.

It's just a short reminder to all of us who are working so hard in life. We should not let time slip through our fingers without having spent it with our children who mean the world to us. If we die tomorrow, the company that we are working for could easily replace us in a matter of days. But the family and friends that we leave behind will feel the loss for the rest of their lives. But unfortunately, most of us pour ourselves more into work than into our families.

Spending a good amount of time should be our goal as fathers, but all of us at some point of time certainly just cannot afford it. But we can always make up for the loss by using a few sure-shot tools that connect us well and also inspire our kids.

Every child should be welcomed into a family with gladness. We should take time to enjoy them, play with them and teach them. A child needs his parents' time more than anything else in the world. The conversation in the story above illustrates that. Spending time with your children is the greatest gifts you can give them. We need to always tell them how special they are and that they mean the world to us.

The secret is to emotionally, mentally and physically be fully present in every moment we spend with our kids, no matter how short these moments are. There are many activities that take very little time but offer wonderful opportunities for bonding. Mentioned below are some examples of things that really take up only a small amount of time and still work wonders in bonding.

The simplest example is giving a bath to the child or changing the diaper. Giving a bath is often seen as something that's almost totally under mother's or nanny's domain in most households. Kids, on the contrary, love to have it from their fathers and often long for it. A warm, relaxing bath given by the dad makes both the kids and the fathers feel great. Helping the kids with brushing and other bathroom chores improves bonding beyond imagination.

I have always been amazed when I see the sign on the door of a public toilet of a woman changing the baby's diaper. Diaper changing is one thing that really instantaneously enhances bonding between the parent and the infant.

###  25. One-Minute Magic

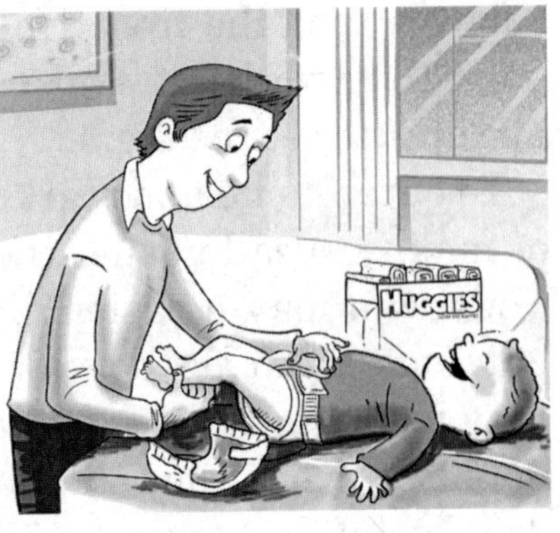


Ask somebody to video-record you changing a diaper and see how you are getting better at it with practice. You can even have a contest with some family friends to find out who does it best. It will do good to only one person – to you! In a study carried out by Huggies, parents described the nappy-changing moments as some of the most memorable ones of their parenting years.

## Crucial Everyday Magic

The beginning and end of our children's day are crucial minutes in parenting. An infant is woken with lots of love and care, so why do we stop doing that when the children grow older? 'I love you' is a phrase our children need more than anything else. Our children need to feel unconditional love to help their self-worth and confidence soar.

My friend Craig Richards, a senior and experienced life coach, works for six months and holidays for the other six. He has four kids and believes that the first five minutes on arriving home from work or travel are the most important minutes to set the scene.

To enter home and start checking your laptop or making a call pushes the whole family away. Your wife may occasionally complain about it, but kids often do not complain, even though they feel equally bad and ignored. The day will not be far when they stop coming running to the door when you come home, and one day, they may not even look at you when you go to their room and you may have to loudly announce your arrival.

###  26. One-Minute Magic

Wake your children up lovingly every day and say, 'Honey! I love you so much. It is going to be a great day today.'

###  27. One-Minute Magic

Set a positive scene as soon as you reach home. Start with a song or a very nice comment. Add some spice to the moment. As the head of the family, your real job starts when you get home in the evening; do it right and your children will look forward to your arrival every day. Most men think that their job is over when they reach home.

###  28. One-Minute Magic

Make bedtime really special for your children. Talk to them. Listen to them. Give them a positive comment. If you have a book of short stories and read a few pages every day with some subtle added message from your side, it is the easiest way to mould their thoughts and behaviours.

#### Do Not Assume

I asked best-selling author and entrepreneur Jay Niblick, author of *What's Your Genius*, to share his most important message for parents. His answer was: 'Do not assume [your children] know that you love them. Make sure you tell them that you love them each and every day. Make sure not to lay any conditions to the love (that we so often routinely do), e.g., if you eat that junky bag of crisps, I am going to really hate you for that. Even if you have to scold and punish them, always end the discussion with, 'You know I love you just as much, regardless of what you did.' If they truly know you love them unconditionally, everything else can be worked out – it has a huge impact on their positive self-esteem.'

Regarding quality time, Jay said, 'The most important thing is to be present.' Being at the dinner table while reading emails on the smartphone is not being present with them really and this is certainly not quality time.

At a family workshop, one of the saddest things once witnessed was when a boy, aged about nine, was asked to name two people who loved him. His father was standing directly behind him but the boy could not come up with a single name. The embarrassed father learned two things:

- His son did not feel loved.
- He needed to do a better job in showing his love for his son.

Let's vow to make sure of just one thing if nothing else – to make our kids firmly believe that we love them.

### Rock-a-bye Baby

Toddlers love to be rocked by their mothers but to be rocked by their fathers is a whole new and wonderful experience for them. Rock your toddlers as often as you can and you will enjoy it as much as they do. Whistling comes naturally, but try and sing to them too.

### Tell 'My bedtime' Story

Occasionally, instead of telling your children bedtime stories, tell them about the time when you were a boy, the sports you played, and what all you did at school. Let them know you were a child once too. Plan what messages you want to convey and then incorporate them in your stories to get it subtly across to them. Most such messages will be etched in their minds for life. They will love hearing the stories from you and will get to know their dad even better.

### Do Not Miss Out

From the time we get back home, we must ensure that we give our full presence to our children.

They just grow up so fast. As poet John Whittier wrote, 'Of all sad words of tongue or pen, the saddest are these: "*It might have been.*"'

We always have a choice in what we do and how we do it.

## Dinner-time Fun

Try to throw a formal dinner party in the middle of the week. Dress up. Teach your children some table manners. It is fun and it polishes their behaviour for formal occasions.

Similarly, you can have a lemonade party. Let your children dress up as adults and serve them cake and punch. These may look like strange suggestions but having met the families who do this regularly, I can tell you that these are the master strokes which have set these families apart as examples.

## Let's Celebrate!

As a family, decide on a goal where improvement is needed. When you have achieved it, celebrate as a family. Throw a victory party, an ice cream party, a water fight, or whatever you all enjoy.

## Incantations / Positive Affirmations

Besides some of the fun activities mentioned above, one serious habit that can be developed while spending time with the children is incantations – these are the most underused tools in our armoury. Incantations are short, affirmative sentences, which are repeated over and over again over weeks and even months. For example, 'Every day, I am getting stronger and stronger'. As mentioned in Chapter 2, this concept about the subconscious mind and encouragement is repeated a few times in the book simply to emphasize its sheer importance and multidimensional facets.

If something is repeated enough, the subconscious mind will eventually accept it as a fact and mould the person accordingly without too much trouble. It is difficult to believe but if you ask any peak-performance athlete or a successful sportsperson what their coach teaches them first, the answer without fail would be: to repeat something so many times that it becomes a part of your nervous system. Muhammad Ali, the famous boxer, says, 'I said I am the most powerful boxer so many times to myself every single day that my brain started believing it and made me achieve it.'

To make the incantations more fun, they should be repeated out loud with the whole family. Another good idea is to write them on a board or print a poster and put them up in a place where they can be seen every day. There is virtually no limit to the incantations one can make, but they have to be positive and realistic. An incantation that says 'I can walk on water' might be fun, but it will not do much good. If I am forty-five years old and say repeatedly, 'I will win the next 100m gold medal,' that wouldn't be much good either, though anything is possible. Instead, a child saying something like 'I am a great public speaker/dancer/athlete' will do him a lot of good and move him towards greatness.

### 29. One-Minute Magic

Some powerful examples of affirmatives that will take only a minute and certainly have a positive effect on the kids' minds are:

- I always do my best.
- I always think before answering.
- I always cooperate with my parents when they need help.
- I practise creativity to keep my mind fresh and intelligent, and to make myself a genius. It makes me feel like a scientist.
- I am respectful and listen carefully to my parents.

- I always keep my promises.
- I speak gently to everybody.
- I am proud to have such a great family.
- I take care of my lovely brother/sister as I am a great brother/sister to him/her.
- I eat only healthy and energizing foods that make my body and brain very strong.
- I always impress myself. (The subtle message here is not to let them become a pleaser who tries to keep everybody happy, which is actually one of the commonest causes of depression and an outcome of low self-worth.)
- I am an outstanding speaker and deliver great speeches.
- I am super intelligent and do all my work brilliantly.

Positive thinking is another quality that needs constant repetition by spending time with kids. Each and every day, parents should encourage their children to think positive rather than to dwell on the negative, and to foster an attitude of thankfulness and be grateful for our many blessings. What parents often don't realize is that *thinking positively can significantly affect their children's future for the better.*

##  30. One-Minute Magic

Tell your kids in the morning, 'It is going to be a great day', and say this every day.

When leaving home, say: 'Remember, your father loves you,' or tell them, 'Your mother and I smile every time we think of you.'

### How This Works

What we focus on is what we create. The brain does not understand the word 'not'. If somebody suggests, *'Try not to spill the milk,'* it just makes the child more prone to do that. Instead, it's better to say, *'Drink your milk slowly. I am proud of you, honey.'*

On a lighter note, tell kids often, 'Have a lot of fun today,' and say this with a big smile on your face. The kids' brains will focus on having fun instead of the small bickering that happens during the day. It is our duty to shift our kids' focus on to the right and positive things that are most important in life.

Many more fun suggestions are enlisted in Chapter 10 titled 'Blast-offs'.

# 5
# Discovering and Developing Talents

Most educational professionals agree that all children have some inherent talents and abilities, which can be identified at an early age. Beethoven composed his greatest music after he became deaf. Demosthenes, one of the greatest orators of all times, overcame a lisp (a type of speech defect) by putting rocks in his mouth and practising hour after hour to overcome it. Olympic gymnasts make the balance beam, the uneven bars and the floor routine look easy. Nothing comes easy. It takes hours and hours of practice and hard work.

In India, we are too focussed on being a doctor or an engineer or training to take over the family business. There is not enough focus on what children's real talents are and if they would indeed be happy pursuing these professions and streams. There is no dearth of people switching streams after decades of work in one field, eventually starting from scratch. Finding and developing those talents does need some time and effort to be spent practising consistently.

I have always admired the wisdom of Ralph Waldo Emerson's words, 'That which we persist in doing becomes easier for us to do; not that the nature of the thing is changed, but that our power to do is increased.'

There are certain questions you can ask your child to help you both discover their gifts and talents. This way you will be able to provide relevant experiences and encouragement along the way.

### 31. One-Minute Magic

Identify your children's gifts by asking questions like the ones suggested below. Write the answers down, don't just leave them in your head – thoughts are like clouds; they disappear, never to come back in the same form. What is written stays.

Ask them to make a list of:

- Three things you think you do well.
- Three things you enjoy doing.
- Three things you would like to learn.

###  32. One-Minute Magic

Complete the following sentences:

- I am happiest when ...
- I am saddest when ...
- I feel good when ...
- I feel joy when ...
- I feel peaceful when ...
- I really desire to have ...

We can use the answers to promote our children's interests, desires and talents. To make this exercise even more powerful, we can add these to the list of incantations. Having incantations that your kids have formulated themselves not only makes them more meaningful for them, it also increases the perceived value of the entire list.

## Developing Natural Talents

Once your children have discovered their talents, they must be willing to invest the time and effort necessary to develop and polish them. Mastery of talent must be earned. A good coach or mentor goes a long way and a father can certainly be one.

Geniuses always do one thing at a time, and they do it really well. If your child is old enough to comprehend, ask your kid, 'If you had all the time and money in the world, what would you love to do or be?'

Probe into their natural strengths by asking if they liked playing with friends, giving a great speech, playing a game, or performing a creative activity. If you encourage them to keep a diary, both your kids and you will see the blueprint of their true selves.

**33. One-Minute Magic**

Ask about the *why, how* and *what* of things, or frame questions like:

- What part of it do you like most?
- What part of it will you enjoy the most?
- What part of it will you not like?
- How do you think it will make you happy?

Give constant and positive support to your children as they develop their talents and skills. Make lessons, books and other resources available when and where it's possible or necessary.

Attend kids' school performances as a family. Give kids special recognition for talks,

winning a debate or a poetry competition. Make them live the future dream now and they will move a lot closer to achieving it.

This also annihilates mediocrity from their system and boosts confidence along with a zest for being really good at whatever they do.

### 36. One-Minute Magic

Get yourself laughed at for something you are not good at. Kids do not mind if their parents are imperfect. On the contrary, they will be far more open to constructive criticism if you adopt this attitude.

### The Art of Drawing

It is great to help kids draw. A picture is worth a thousand words. The human brain has two halves – the leftbrain is the logical side and the right is the creative part of our thinking, including imagination, intuition, etc. Drawing a picture is a simple deal. It activates the right side of the brain and develops their creativity and imagination.

### 37. One-Minute Magic

Suggest to your kids, 'How about drawing your joyous face after you win a dance, debate or competition while your daddy is watching you?' This not only stimulates the creative brain but the child also envisions success in greater detail. This keeps their tender yet powerful minds on the right track, working towards their future, and makes them do things and take concrete steps towards their goals. Say to your kids, 'Let us draw what your own house will look like when you are a parent.'

Put your children's drawings on a wall, on the fridge, or in your office. Let them know how happy their drawings make you every day and they will also remind them of their new goals.

### Creative Thinking for Kids

Ask the kids to write a list of what qualities in life they want to have in themselves, for example, being healthy, feeling loved, having fun, being a guitar player, etc.

Ask them to repeat this fun activity of making the list each year, roughly around the same day. The list will change hugely as they grow, but there will always be some very interesting things in it. This improves their ability to set goals early in life, and even if they do not achieve them completely, the focus is always in the right direction. Research has shown that good goal setters are the top achievers.

### The Quality of Observation

Keen observation is an asset. Successful people are able to observe things and spot opportunities when others are not. This is a quality that can be developed at a very early age. For example, when you get back from shopping, ask them to write down (just like a surprise test) every possible kids' items they can remember having seen. Initially, they might not be able to mention many, but the list can go to hundreds of items like toys, games, cartoon characters, stickers, new toys stocked in the store that they have noticed on the last visit, and so on.

## 38. One-Minute Magic

Make a special trip out. Go to the park, shop or take a walk in your neighbourhood. On your return, ask your kids to try to make a list of all the fun things they saw from A to Z. Take turns and enjoy the fun of the day. By the way, this strategy is also used to train management executives to understand and develop the value of keen observation. It programmes the kids to be more observant of their surroundings.

## 39. One-Minute Magic

Take a nature walk with your child if there are special places near your home such as a forest or seashore, the mountains or a desert, and point out how beautiful things are.

After your walk, encourage your child to make a nature's collage. Some pictures, for example, of a dried leaf, flower or seashell could be added to it. Let your child choose. The purpose is to appreciate nature and that will happen with this activity.

### Developing Imagination

Using building blocks in a new way, creating different buildings and shapes or just asking kids to create what they like stimulates imagination. The simple things make all the difference. Kids have the capability to develop detailed ideas faster than adults. During the first ten years, the right brain, which is responsible for creativity, is the dominant conscious force. With a bit of help, this creativity can easily be nurtured into a lasting and powerful part of a child's being.

Get some old cartons, boxes, paper and strings – anything you have lying around – and create models of buildings or monuments in the world. It might be the Eiffel Tower, the Statue of Liberty, Dad's office block, or your home. Whatever it is, it will be rewarding fun.

I know what you are going to say now – this doesn't last a minute!!! Even though it may take more than a minute to build, motivating your kids in the process will not take longer than a minute.

### Sense of Humour

Kids with a well-developed sense of humour are happier and more optimistic, have higher self-esteem, and can handle differences (their own and others') well. Kids who can appreciate and share humour are better liked by their peers and more able to handle adversities. Laughing together is a way to connect and a good sense of humour can also make kids smarter, healthier and better able to cope with challenges.

Make it a point to have at least one good laugh a day as a family. Humour binds people more than anything else and lightens the atmosphere. One of the easiest ways is, of course, to make fun of yourself.

### 40. One-Minute Magic

At the end of the day, talk about one silly thing you did in the day so everybody laughs out loud, including yourself. Not only does the child become a better communicator with his parents about wrongs that he feels he has done, he also develops a better sense of humour, a stronger and more positive attitude and an ability to deal with any situation.

Developing a healthy variety of skills will ensure that your child will be successful in many walks of life and not just academics.

### 41. One-Minute Magic

Play the 'silly old me' game. Have the family guess what was the silliest thing you did at home today, last week or ever. They'll love you more for your honesty and will love to admit theirs more easily in future. What can be a simpler way to have your kids open up?

### Teaching Goal-setting

The power of goal-setting is far superior in children to that of adults. Ask any kid what he wants and he will immediately enumerate a list of things that he wants for Christmas or his birthday. When adults are asked to list five things they want in life, they not only struggle, but also have no idea of quantity, time frame or quality. And that is why they rarely achieve their goals. Give the gift of this invaluable ability to your kids. It will serve them throughout their lives. Kids associate men with planning, so they will love doing this with you.

Did you know that according to research only 2 to 3 per cent of the population writes down their goals? Ninety per cent of those who do, however, are the ones who achieve them.

Get together with your kids and ask them to write down their goals or 'wish list' for the next month, year, and possibly for the next five years. Discuss the list and then put it away in a safe place. Set a date to revise it. This is an exercise to give hope and get their creative minds thinking. Revisit your children's 'wish list' every month for a minute and discuss it. Is it the same? Has it changed? If yes, why?

A high self-worth is the ultimate gift that parents can give to their child which in return would prove mutually rewarding in later years.

## Set Some Goals Together

Create a family life list or one for each member, if desired. Include as many things as possible you may want to do during the next few weeks to years. Take turns in talking about the lists and encourage the family to work together to achieve the goals. Someone might say he wants to ride a horse or go for a balloon ride. These goals trigger great family adventures and ambitions and make the family a more cohesive unit where all support one another and raise everybody's standards.

# 6
# Inculcating Self-Worth

One of the key factors that finally made me take the plunge to write this book is the story I share below. The essence of being a super dad is that our kids feel special in our company as they are growing and eventually feel great about themselves all the time, as they walk through life. That's what a good boss, a good employer, a good teacher and a good coach are supposed to achieve, and very often, we are able to play these roles to perfection but don't take the home role as seriously. Although we have discussed encouragement and some bits of self-worth in earlier chapters, some aspects need further discussion.

Self-worth is the pivot to a successful life. As the child grows, it will be his most powerful friend that will let him be resourceful even in thin times.

## A Father's Worst Nightmare

On 29 July 2012, my dear friend and inspirational speaker, Gary King, while on a speaking tour in Australia, got a call that his only biological son, Jason King, had jumped off a bridge in Florida and committed suicide. Jason was forty at that time and had been battling depression for years. It was heart-wrenching.

Despite being an inspirational speaker for kids and travelling around the world, Gary had struggled with his own son for years. During the first few years of Jason's life, Gary was extremely busy with his career and made great success and progress. He overlooked the importance of building a connection with his son, Jason, and never really connected with him.

Jason developed a severe lack of self-worth and a feeling of not being enough. By the time Gary realized this, Jason was well into his teens and despite his hardest and most sincere efforts, Gary could never connect back with him.

Such a loss is any parent's worst nightmare. How could a father ever recover? There is nothing worse than thinking we could have done something differently. Remorse is the worst feeling one can have.

[This story has been mentioned with due permission from Gary who does not want any other father to go through the same. Today, Gary wants to help teenaged kids struggling with depression and suicidal tendencies. He has since helped many parents. Most suicides can be traced back to a strained connection or lack of it with the father/mother in some way or the other.]

Though Jason's real-life story is an extreme case, less severe or subtle things that happen to our kids often go unnoticed causing them lifetime complexes, phobias, distress and depression that we fail to even recognize.

My mission in writing this book is to not just prevent such awful events from happening to our kids, but to equip and empower the readers (particularly dads) with small methods that will make a huge difference in the quality of their relationship with their kids, thereby enhancing the quality of both their own and their kids' lives. A suicide is the last resort of a person who has lost all self-worth and sees no hope for a future.

Self-worth determines practically every decision we make, because our nature is to stay consistent with our identity. An identity is just a set of beliefs we have about ourselves. Our relationships, our career and even our financial stability are all based on how we define who we are. Self-worth helps us to forgive, to be honest, and to feel grateful. It also protects us from unhealthy addictions and builds emotional immunity. A healthy self-worth serves a person for life and can help him breeze through any kind of hardship or suffering.

Low self-worth is an out-of-control epidemic today in India, especially with stressed, overworked teachers in classrooms shouting and punishing students for anything and everything. It is an insidious disease, brought about by believing that we are 'not enough'. And it is going untreated. Low self-worth is at the root of almost all human suffering: stress, anger, obsession, addiction, money problems, disease and dozens of other situations, including wars. A person with great self-worth is not arrogant. Such a person is actually the most humble.

Every day, our children are bombarded with images that imply they need something or the other to feel complete. Power and money have become the defining measures of self-worth today, whereas the reality is just the opposite. Recollect how your kid feels when you deny him a tablet while his friends have one, or when you refuse to download an app that you do not feel is right for him.

Never allow your children to believe they are not enough. Never ever! We should try our best to see that our children develop a high self-worth. Happiness is not something to be chased or pursued, but something that we can have simply by giving ourselves permission to be happy. Teach your kids the same.

Like charity, teaching effective self-worth begins at home. As parents, it is our responsibility to teach our children that they mean the world to us. Every child should be made to feel that he is loved and he deserves it. A high self-worth is the ultimate gift that parents can give to their child, which in return would prove mutually rewarding.

## 42. One-Minute Magic

Take a small jar. Stick a label on it: 'The Hooray Jar'. Every time your kids do something praiseworthy, write it down on a piece of paper and put it in the jar. Once a week, gather everyone around and read out all the good deeds they have done and reward them with praise. Your children will want to do more good things even with little or no further effort from you.

## 43. One-Minute Magic

Teach your children a 'We are great' song and sing it whenever the atmosphere needs a boost of happiness. It could be:

> We are great, we are great; we are special as can be,
> It is great, it is great, to be a family,
> For we have learned to get along, so let us not make a fuss,
> We are great, we are great; we are happy to be happy to be,
> Happy to be us.

Motivate them to write their own version of this song and help them make up their own family tune.

## One-Minute Grenades

Most of us say nasty and hurtful things to our children when we are angry or not in the right frame of mind. Frustrations can so easily overtake us. This is unfair and harmful for our kids' self-worth. Therefore, never say:

- 'You cannot ever do anything right.'
- 'Typical of you to do it wrong.'
- 'Let me do it, you just cannot do it right.'
- 'You are so dumb.'
- 'Why can you not learn this?'
- 'Why are you so useless?'
- 'You are in the way.'
- 'Why can you not be more like ...?'
- 'Not now, I am busy.'
- 'Go away.'

## Some Activities Boosting Self-worth

- At bedtime, during different nights of the week, spend some time with each child to express how much he/she means to you.

- Hold a family council once a week to discuss upcoming projects. Include the whole family in the decision-making process to help your children feel involved, worthwhile and loved.

### 44. One-Minute Magic

Tell your kids something special when you tuck them in bed at night. Here are some samples:

- 'You are so important.'
- 'You are absolutely lovable and capable of doing great things.'
- 'I would hike a thousand miles for you.'
- 'You are such a hard worker. I love you.'
- 'You are so special.'
- 'You practise for your piano lessons very well.'
- 'I am so glad that you are my son/daughter.'
- 'I am happy to have you.'
- 'You always stay strong and healthy because you eat healthy.'
- 'I wish my body was flexible like yours.'
- 'You are going to have some lovely dreams today.'
- 'You have a great dressing sense.'

Show your child a picture of him as a newborn baby. Describe how you felt when you saw, held and loved that baby for the first time.

## Tending the Loving Buds

The most important thing we can teach our children is that they are loved—unconditionally. It is not just the belief in love that is important; it is the atmosphere that goes with it. It is crucial for our children to feel loved and to be fuelled by great values and integrity.

I knew a gardener who grew the most beautiful flowers I had ever seen. One day, I asked him what his secret was. His reply was, 'I stay close to the garden. I go into my garden every day, even when it is not convenient. While I am there, I look for small signs of possible problems, like weeds, insects or bad soil conditions. If caught in time, it's easy to correct them but if left unchecked, these will become overwhelming.'

Children are like young, tender plants. They need love and special care. They need a gentle but firm hand to train and guide them if they are to blossom fully. If we want our precious plants to grow, we must stay close to them and go into the garden every day, even when it is not convenient. As fathers, we need to be on the lookout for the little problems and when we see them, we need to deal with those straight away before they become bigger.

A child must be appreciated for every success, no matter how small and, if possible, it should be celebrated to get his mind to want more of it and work towards that with more confidence and belief in himself; in other words, for him to hone his self-worth. A good and strong sense of self-worth is like the constantly running background software which keeps all other processes in synchrony, ensuring success and happiness for the growing child.

While spending time with your children, share King Louis' story to let them know that they are heaven-sent:

> Before King Louis went to prison, he taught his son, the prince, that he was born to be a king. The men who had removed the king wanted to destroy the boy's sense of right and wrong by teaching him bad habits so that he would never become a great leader.
>
> The prince was exposed to every wicked and unclean thing imaginable ... rich and harmful foods, vulgar language, dishonesty, wickedness and corruption.

Six months later, the prince had not given in to any of these temptations.

When questioned why he had not given into such 'desirable' things, the prince said, 'I cannot do what you ask, for I am born to be a king.' (Source: 'The King's Son', New Era, November 1975, p.35.)

The message of the story is that if we instil a strong sense of self-worth in our children and make them believe they are special from the earliest possible age, their chance of falling into bad habits becomes significantly less.

## Unconditional Love: Do They Know It?

Sometimes, we can be thoughtless and even cruel to the people we love the most. It is often easier to be kind to people we hardly know than to our own family members. If used wrongly, our thoughts, words and actions can turn into powerful weapons of destruction.

Telling your children you love them is of course important, but it is *even more important to show them that you do.* This is psychological!

One father told me, 'One day, when I was really engrossed in finishing off a report, my four-year-old son was trying to get my attention. I told him, "Son, I love you a lot." Unimpressed, he replied, "I do not want you to love me. I want you to play football with me."'

Spend time with your kids – it will make all the difference now and in the future. It is the most significant way we prove the magical words 'I love you.'

## 45. One-Minute Magic

Always say what you mean and mean what you say. 'I will always love you, no matter what.' Never say such words if you do not mean them. Kids are natural psychologists and can make out if what you are saying is true or not. If they feel you don't mean what you say, they might stop trusting you.

## 46. One-Minute Magic

Look into their eyes and say, 'All I want is for you to be strong, happy and successful.' Kids love to hear this. Find opportunities to say it time and again and say it with utmost sincerity and not out of routine.

These simple and ordinary suggestions have worked for hundreds of parents across the globe to bring about great results. The key secret is consistency in being mindful and present.

###  47. One-Minute Magic

Explain, 'We all make mistakes. When you make a mistake and I scold you, it does not mean I do not love you. It just means I do not approve of such behaviour.' Be specific in mentioning the behaviour, if possible.

###  48. One-Minute Magic

While helping kids with any chores, homework or problems, say sincerely, 'Because I love you, I will always help you.' And it should come from the heart.

###  49. One-Minute Magic

Make up a family song, even a few lines will do, don't bother being perfect. Sing it often. The words will stick long and powerfully in the memory of children and they will cherish it for the rest of their lives.

###  50. One-Minute Magic

When back from work, smile and say, 'I really missed you all day today.' The first few minutes of entering home in the evening are critically important.

###  51. One-Minute Magic

Lift your kid up often and say, 'I am so lucky to have a son/daughter like you.' Your presence in my life makes it so much more beautiful. The words will help your kids' confidence soar. *It cannot be this simple*, you may be thinking. But almost always, it's the small and simple things that bring us closer, provided they are done consistently and diligently.

## Increasing Family Love and Togetherness

Your getting involved in their activities shows your children how important they really are to you. Going on a family walk together is a great way where many unexpected things candidly come out in the open.

###  52. One-Minute Magic

Point out things like a sweater or a hat that grandmother knitted for them and say, 'It took hours for your grandmother to make this for you. She must love you very much.'

###  53. One-Minute Magic

Remind them of a gift or a compliment that they received from a friend/relative and add some details to make them feel important.

### 54. One-Minute Magic

Show them a bird's nest and say, 'We can learn a lesson in love by watching the mother bird bring food to the baby birds. Their mother loves them so much.'

### 55. One-Minute Magic

Build a collection of happy photos of your family and children that you can all enjoy seeing together now and then. These days, with smartphones, a themed album of photos can always be at our fingertips. A collection of ten to twelve photos is ideal. The subconscious mind will tune in to the shared wavelength and pick up a positive feeling in just a few seconds. This action shifts the brain into a state of gratitude and joy to focus on the great things around us. In that state, we will always get the right ideas and be more balanced. Sharing such memories repeatedly with our children often enforces a lot of positive things.

### 56. One-Minute Magic

When your kids feel discouraged, tell them to look in a mirror and say, 'I am important. I matter. I can learn and grow. I can be kind to others. I can succeed.' Andrew Carnegie, one of the first self-made millionaires in the history would spend five minutes in front of the mirror every morning, saying such stuff to himself. He trained his workers to do the same exercise in the mirror every day and though it looked ordinary, it changed their mindset to achieve greatness. This is a part of positive imaging. We become what we constantly and consistently think about.

### 57. One-Minute Magic

Give children several note cards and ask them to write on each card, 'I am lovable and capable. I am becoming more ...' And here the words could be 'loving', 'kind', 'patient', 'forgiving', 'educated', 'generous', etc. Make sure the cards are always handy, so that they can be easily reviewed, even at the breakfast table.

###  58. One-Minute Magic

Play the *'who blinks first'* game. Staring is a great way to increase bonding and love. This works almost every time with almost all children. Make sure you smile and emit love as you stare.

### Good Fairy Activities

Remember the excitement we felt when we lost a baby tooth, slipped the tooth under the pillow and waited for the tooth fairy to bring a surprise. Why do we restrict the fun and wait to lose a tooth for such surprises?

To reinforce good behaviour, introduce the good fairy on other occasions too. When you see something that deserves a small reward, then say, 'Congratulations! You did so well that the good fairy is going to put a surprise under your pillow tonight.'

The good fairy can gift a note, treats, pencils – whatever you like – that night. Children will start looking for good and positive things to do, so they can have the good fairy treat.

### 59. One-Minute Magic

Show interest in how your daughter looks and dresses. Little comments like, 'your hairclip looks great in this way' will mean the world to her. It may sound a bit too simple or possibly silly at first, but do try it out.

Tell her, 'How come you look so pretty and energetic even at the end of the day?' Compliments will always bring a smile on her face and make her feel more confident.

### 60. One-Minute Magic

When travelling, send your kids a one-minute videotext saying how much you miss them. (If they don't have their own phone, you could send it to your partner and have her show it to them.) It will show them a lot more love from you, even when you're having a day of uninvolved presence at home.

### 61. One-Minute Magic

Help your kid start the day with positive, loving feelings. You could have a one-minute dance on your daughter's favourite track with her when she feels like it. It will make her happy, wake her body up, and give her a beautiful memory for the whole day and beyond.

### 62. One-Minute Magic

Show that you value their knowledge and opinion by asking questions like, 'Can you tell me what/why/how ...?' They will feel proud that their dad seeks their advice.

Take your daughter out for a 'Daddy – Daughter Date'. Talk and do whatever is fun.

### 63. One-Minute Magic

To relive positive events, have a one-minute memory session on why was it a great day yesterday. Ask your kids about their friends and how they are getting on with them. Friends and the 'not-so-good' friends are a critical issue in their lives, especially for daughters. Girls think a lot but rarely speak about their thoughts to parents and if their dad guides them a bit on how to have better relations, it is a huge support and help.

**Praying Together**

A family that prays together, stays together – this saying is indeed true. Introducing spiritual practices to your children when they are young lets them view praying as a natural part of life and allows you, as a parent and caregiver, to have a spiritual influence on them before other people do.

Spirituality can connect kids to the divine, to each other and to the past. If you're raising your child in the same spiritual tradition that you were raised in, be sure he knows that he's carrying on family rituals that were passed along by his grandparents and even great-grandparents.

Religion and spirituality should be more joyful than sombre and serious. Encourage your children to draw a picture of God, write their own story about how the world came to be, or simply imagine what heaven looks like. Together, act out plays or put on a puppet show based on creation stories or your own spiritual themes.

# 7
# Role Models

Kids spend only one-eighth of the year in school and the rest outside it. Home is their most important environment and they spend seven-eighths of a year there, which makes it a place of immense opportunity for parents. This fact came as a great revelation to me, as we keep expecting teachers and schools to inculcate things which parents can do far better. Moreover, kids always look up to their parents, who are their first role models. This chapter offers some ideas on setting an example for them and snippets on some other topics that we need to speak or educate them about at a very young age.

Any human will morph consciously, and more importantly subconsciously, into the type of people he most often meets, interacts or spends his time with.

When we wish to teach our children specific values, we can do it best by example. We can easily be their first and most inspiring role models, unless we choose not to be.

Parenting is a skill that can be acquired, honed and nurtured, one that needs some self discipline too, as there is a tender mind observing it all. When you do something consistently, kids get a strong message that it is okay, even if it is not. This can mean doing something, like smoking and shouting, as well as *not* doing something, for example *not* cleaning up after creating a mess.

As children observe far more than we do, we should explain to them repeatedly and subtly that fathers too are humans and sometimes fail to set a proper example. Sometimes we get tired, feel discouraged, or lose our tempers. But we continue to love them and try our best to be good fathers though we do make mistakes.

As discussed before, the left (logical) part of the brain of a child is not developed fully until the age of ten and kids are mostly right (creative) brain dominant. They cannot make out right from wrong until they learn it by experience and observation. If your children are taught to lie *for* you, they will soon be lying *to* you. Be careful what you ask them to do. Even answering the doorbell and saying that you are not at home is a clear sign to the child that lies are acceptable. We must remember that we are the most important people in our children's lives. We are their mentors and the first people they look up to.

Quality solutions come from asking quality questions. You need to ask yourself when your children learned from you just by the way you related to them or when you were not trying to teach them anything in particular.

Below are some examples of this kind of introspection:

- One dad reflects: 'I was out shopping with my toddler, Arjun, and he threw a terrible tantrum. It took about ten minutes to settle him down. When we went home, I set him down for his nap and reflected on the awful scene in the store. Suddenly it dawned on me. He had only been mirroring recent tensions at home as I was not getting on well with my colleague at office and was a bit relentless at home.'
- Another dad writes: 'I almost choked on my dinner when my seven-year-old son asked if

he could have a cigarette. 'Absolutely not!' I answered indignantly. He said, 'But why not, Dad? You smoke all the time.' What could I say? He was right. It was in those few moments that I realized that it is not so much what we say to our children, but what we do.'

### Smoking is Injurious to Health

Second-hand/passive smoke is dangerous for anyone, more particularly for children. It increases the likelihood of Sudden Infant Death Syndrome (SIDS), asthma, lower respiratory tract infections and other health problems. The alarming thing is that half of children aged 4–11 are exposed to second-hand smoke in some form, whether it is sporadically inhaled in public places or regularly at home.

More crucially, their tender minds are led to believe that smoking is acceptable and they are subsequently far easier prey to drugs and addictions in the future. The tobacco and alcohol companies do the rest with their shrewd and clever advertising and influence.

There are small things that we can do or say that will trigger their minds to think about it, and it is most effectively done by setting an example for them. Below are some such suggestions.

### 64. One-Minute Magic

Say, 'Let us stay away from things that might hurt or make us sick. Let us eat fruits and vegetables, so that we can be strong.' Following up the discussion in the next few days with a few meals predominantly made of these food groups will help drive home the point.

### 65. One-Minute Magic

Ask children for their ideas on how to have a happy family and an orderly house. Then try to make your behaviour a role model for their ideas. Randomly tidying up a few things in the days to follow reinforces and registers the point.

### 66. One-Minute Magic

When going out for a large social gathering/ party, e.g., a wedding or birthday bash, pretend to be making new friends apart from the ones already known. Ask them to make at least one new friend per outing. Say, 'Today you will make one new friend during this event and then we can have fun talking about how it went.'

##  67. One-Minute Magic

Put money into a donation box in front of your kids and tell them how important charity is in life. Tell your kids what happens with the money and how other people who are less fortunate can benefit from even the smallest gesture. Even better, when you see a donation box read the label to your kids and ask them if they want to help that cause. Most of the time, kids will say 'yes' and then you can give them money and let them put it into the box. This not only teaches them the value of charity, it also gives your kids the joy of having helped someone. Your kids can then tell their friends or family that they have done a charitable donation and how it affected someone's life. It takes less than a minute and is such a rewarding experience.

###  One-Minute Grenade

Giving in to tantrums only communicates *tantrum = reward*. Try to walk away from a tantrum. No child likes to throw a tantrum without an audience. Once he is a bit more receptive, try and sit with him and make him mull over things together with you.

One effective way for us to teach our children about love and bonding is by demonstrating our love to their mother/their grandparents in front of them as often as we can.

### Lend Your Ear

An important way of passing our values to children is to *listen* to them. When we listen to them, they learn to listen to us. Encourage your children to come to you with their problems. Discuss important matters with them. By doing this frequently from a young age onwards, they will come to you first, rather than seeking somebody outside the family for advice, which could get them into trouble and will often create distance between them and the family.

Ask yourself:

- Do I really listen to each family member?
- Do I spend quality time alone with each member of the family?
- Do I express and show my belief in each family member?

A simple, yet highly effective gift is to listen more than talk. Most people have lost interest in listening. They pretend to listen while they either think about what they want to say next or about something completely different. And while most adults do not even notice this, because they are doing the same, children pick up on it immediately and lose interest in communicating with that person. Listening truly is one of the greatest gifts you can give to your child.

## Be Smart with Money

Money is an important topic in life, often not taught to kids properly until they are adults. It is, however, paramount to instil some understanding and skills right from a very young age, in understanding its importance.

For some, it may mean living within one's means, for some others who are richer, it means understanding the value of money and not getting things too easily which helps realize their value. My friend, Sharon Lechter, shared her wisdom on this. She is the co-author of *Rich Dad, Poor Dad* and an ex-member of a former US president's advisory council on financial literacy. She says: 'I encourage everyone to be an entrepreneur, even if you are an employee. You can become entrepreneurial-minded within your own job ... Learn to go the extra mile. The bottom line is being accountable, responsible, and having a clear vision in whatever you are doing in your life.'

## 68. One-Minute Magic

Encourage your kids to turn off the lights when they are not using a room, by saying, 'We can save some power and money too. Let us conserve our resources.' It is important that they respect the resources and facilities we have and use them mindfully without wastage.

## 69. One-Minute Magic

Encourage them to live within the available money by saying, 'We never go over our credit limit. That just costs us more money and can get us into a lot of trouble and embarrassment.' It is a good idea to talk about credit and debit cards and explain the difference, whilst out shopping with kids. Credit is a very crucial topic for kids to understand at an early age.

## 70. One-Minute Magic

Ask for discounts or deals while shopping and involve the kids. It is fun! 'Haggle often, even for the smallest deal,' says Sir Richard Branson. If a billionaire like him does it, we certainly should have no hesitation in doing so. When buying something on sale or on discount, explain to kids the meaning of that and how smart planning and timing can regularly save money.

## 71. One-Minute Magic

Involve your kids in budgeting small things. Say, 'How much do you think we should spend on this?' Things like the next electronic item in the house or even smaller things can be discussed. Even if we, as parents, are almost certain of which model/version we will go for, the kids can be brought to agree to that. In essence, it is making a role model of teamwork and communicating that you care.

## 72. One-Minute Magic

Discuss business ideas with your children by just dropping an idea. It helps to activate their creative financial and entrepreneurial skills. The intention behind such discussions and exercises is not to have them start businesses, but to impress upon them how to think, develop and gestate good ideas. Discussing inspirational stories of people who changed the world triggers positive conformity.

A friend of mine who is an author has an eight-year-old child who is starting to write a book on 'How to Keep the Class Teacher Happy'.

##  73. One-Minute Magic

Be direct, but always positive. For example, there will be occasions where you must say no even if your child really needs something. Maybe your child wants to get an expensive toy that a friend just got. Instead of just declining the request, you could say: 'This time, we will not buy that toy. And with the money we save, we can go for a picnic in the park next weekend!' As long as your child loves picnics, this will give a positive flavour to the answer. If there's some other preference that may work better for your child, the same can be articulated.

Adding a positive spin to anything is always a great idea. Especially with your child, it can be the difference between tears and a smile.

### Making Mistakes

When you make a mistake, apologize, admit it and re-declare how you will try to be a better dad. Say, 'I am sorry. I was wrong. Will you forgive me?'

Sorry is a word that can heal many hurts if it is authentic and comes from the heart. It also makes the kids more open to accepting mistakes done by others. Teaching your child that 'it's okay to be wrong sometimes' is a powerful skill for life.

### 74. One-Minute Magic

Ask them once a week, 'Is there anything I did not do right or was unfair about recently. Please suggest what I can do to make it better.' Kids will just ask for a small compensation like a candy or just time together and attention. It makes the kids feel really cared for and loved, and they are unlikely to remember the wrong done.

### 75. One-Minute Magic

When kids make a mistake, hug and say, 'I love you no matter who is right or wrong.' We are setting an example of forgiveness and bonding with the family, and to encourage that admitting mistakes is a great thing in a family, which can help and support you to leave that behind and move forward.

### 76. One-Minute Magic

Speak on a random topic for a minute or so to educate them about it. Ask them to prepare a one-minute speech on a topic like 'my favourite dress/game/toy'. Find other topics that interest them and you will open up their locked thoughts and talents. The skill of making extempore and spot speeches is a great skill that goes a long way in developing effective persuasion and public speaking skills, needed to articulate one's thoughts whilst being respectful of others' opinions and beliefs.

## Manners and Becoming a Role Model

'Do as I say, not as I do' has always been a risky parenting strategy, and this is particularly true when teaching children etiquette. Teaching good manners is essential in raising polite children. Young children are learning from their parents' interactions with their spouse and other family members, as well as from their exchanges with the outside world. So you need to be careful about your manners. Children are great mimics and if you begin to use good manners yourselves, your children are just going to follow suit.

###  77. One-Minute Magic

Ask permission from your children and give them permission:

- 'May I use your paper?'
- 'Yes, my love, you may play with your friend.'

###  78. One-Minute Magic

Always ask and never demand: use 'Would you?' and 'Will you?' This was one of the principal factors Andrew Carnegie, the steel tycoon, attributed his success to. He never ever ordered an employee of his, no matter what. He would always say, 'Would you please mind doing this?' This teaches the importance of respecting people around us.

###  79. One-Minute Magic

When asked for advice, start by saying 'Thank you for asking. With the experience that I have, I think that ....' The point to be subtly made is that you are there to help and are not pushing your opinion. Being a bit tactful and considerate goes a long way and if we can inculcate this into our kids, they will be refined human beings. A good point needs to be conveyed in the right way to be well understood and followed.

###  80. One-Minute Magic

Some situations need a quick explanation or a simple reasoning only. Use brief explanations for certain issues unless a detailed one is needed. Your child will respond better. For example, if your child wants to eat sweets before a meal, just convey that he can have it later in the day, as it is not healthy to have it before the meal. Then change the topic. If you get into a discussion about this, you lose. Either your child comes up with surprisingly brilliant reasons that disarm you, or he leaves the scene upset or crying. Keep it short and you stand a better chance to win.

## 81. One-Minute Magic

Acknowledge the smallest good acts of any family member and praise lavishly and generously, setting an example of appreciating and acknowledging. For example, say, 'That was so nice of you to share it with your sister.'

## 82. One-Minute Magic

In your family time, offer help to your wife and say aloud, 'We are a great team.' The kids pick that up and want to start being a part of the family team culture. Always praise good behaviour by saying, 'I love the way you do/finish your work ...' Also begin your sentences with 'Let us' as these two words rarely fail to work. They instil a spirit of teamwork and always get even the most difficult and lazy children to contribute.

### 83. One-Minute Magic

When you have a tough choice to make, allow the children to see how you work through the problem, weigh the pros and cons, and come to a decision. The process of making a good decision is a skill. A good role model will not only show a child which decision is the best but also how to come to that conclusion. That way, the child will be able to apply that reasoning when they are in a similar situation.

### 84. One-Minute Magic

Eating together is a great way for families to grow together. Use mealtimes as an ideal opportunity to open a new discussion. You can find out what your children know or feel about certain topics – and you have a chance to voice your opinion. For example, talking about the new series of a reality show can start a debate on the pros and cons of reality TV, and what it brings the contestants, how it might affect them, why we find it intriguing ...

### 85. One-Minute Magic

Offer to have a quick hand wrestle with elbows on the table. Pretend to lose at least half of the time. Say, 'You must be doing lots of stuff to keep so strong, I am sure you are eating very well and exercising regularly.' The kid's mind is subtly triggered to keep up the reputation.

## Addictions

Addictions commonly start as a lack of support in life or trying to emulate a wrong role model if the parents are not strong enough role models. Often, kids prefer conforming to peers. If parents show strong support and involvement, addictions are very unlikely. Do not postpone the discussion until your kids have taken to smoking and drinking. Use some One-Minute Magics.

The most important influence is the example we set them as parents. No amount of communication will impress the kids to not try drugs if you have been puffing and drinking in front of them. It is important to guide and inspire our kids and talk about addictions at an early stage so that both their conscious and subconscious minds understand this. What I have learned from some of the fathers I have interviewed is that nothing fulfilled them as much as the fact that their kids had strong ethics and high morale. This does not happen by chance. Success is a planned process, not a coincidence.

Smoking kills more people around the world than all other drug addictions combined. Yet, it is legal. Nicotine is the most addictive substance known to humankind. Eighty per cent of consumer decisions are founded on emotion, not on logic. That is why tobacco and alcohol companies pay huge amounts of money to the media to showcase these substances subtly. Film stars are paid hefty amounts of money to smoke in key scenes that leave a lasting impression. This constant brainwashing deeply affects the subconscious mind, especially since the 'role models' do it.

###  86. One-Minute Magic

Talk of a friend/relative who has a healthy, strong body and is not into any addictions. It helps if your kids likes him and preferably the best way to start is with some subtle suggestions when you are just back from meeting him or he has just left your house after visiting you. Talk about how healthy he is. If you do not have any such friend/relative, make one up and tell the kids, 'you know I have a friend who ...' Talking of him a few times will create a clear mental picture of him in the kids' minds and because you appreciate the friend so much and so often, your kids would be intrigued and jealous of him. Their brains would want to emulate him.

##  87. One-Minute Magic

Say to your kids, 'We love our bodies. We will never abuse them.' This, by the way, is also a great incantation/affirmation.

Explain to them the dangers of addictions by pointing out how they affect other people as well. Say, 'That man does not enjoy smoking his cigarette. He is just not able to get out of the trap.' There are some things, my love, which you have to say no to not only the first time, but every time.

# 8

# Teaching Them Gratitude

Gratitude is appreciating blessings and kindnesses bestowed upon us. We can express it through sincere words of thanks and actions. An increased spirit of gratitude will bring increased joy into our lives.

We should be grateful for what we have been blessed with and teach our kids the same. Our brain is far more complex and capable than we appreciate. Dr Joe Dispenza, a noted brain expert, reveals that the only state in which our conscious and subconscious minds are fully aligned is a state of gratitude. Our brains cannot feel gratitude and stress at the same time. What would you rather choose?

Because gratitude nourishes the soul, elevates mood, charges one emotionally and releases endorphins, we should teach our kids at least one minute of gratitude every day. It is so quick and easy. I like to think of it as fast food for the soul.

## 88. One-Minute Magic

Make a one-minute video about the gratitude you feel for your children and watch it together once in a while.

A friend of mine, Raj, got a specific toy electric car that his son has been asking and looking for everywhere. His son had been literally praying for it for a few weeks. On seeing it, his son was so ecstatic that he told him that he wanted to thank God for it.

Raj recorded a video, which turned out to be really emotional. Watching such videos with the family makes children relive the memory of success and their prayer being answered. The habit to develop and inculcate is to celebrate even the smallest successes.

## 89. One-Minute Magic

Provide a 'Gratitude Diary' for your children. Ask them to spend a minute writing down what they are grateful for every day and do the same yourself, or ask them to make a routine to write down five new things they learned that day.

You can review it on a weekly basis with them, if pressed for time.

### 90. One-Minute Magic

At bedtime, say, 'Tell me five things you are grateful for today.'

### 91. One-Minute Magic

During a meal, invite your children to share something they feel grateful for, anything whatsoever. The purpose is to consistently and repeatedly instil the habits of remembering the blessings in life. Spend a minute asking kids, 'What made today special for you?' Tell them to be specific. This makes them revisit the events of the day and anchor the positive experience.

This is a great way to build family memories and create a stronger bond.

### 92. One-Minute Magic

When praying together, encourage them to be simply thankful to God, for what they are already blessed with. You can even suggest a few things they are so lucky to have in their life.

# 9

# Music: Nutrient of Mind and Body

Music is such an important part of every kid's life that it deserves a separate small chapter. This may be a topic that you simply skip but the effect of music in family life is really deep.

There is nothing else that can affect our health, brain development, behavioural patterns, intelligence and well-being as positively as music. Edwin Coppard, author of *Your Voice Is the Messenger of Your Soul*, says that every person naturally sings from birth onwards, but at some point, he stops. In most cases, it is because of a comment received by a dear one on his imperfect singing abilities. Do not let that happen to your children.

##  93. One-Minute Magic

Sing as much as you can in front of your kids and encourage them to sing as well. Singing is one of the easiest ways to change the mood of people and as long as you choose happy songs, you almost certainly bring a smile to your kid's face. No matter how good or bad a singer we are, the point is not to turn it into a competition, but rather to have fun. In fact, you can sing really badly on purpose just to make them feel at ease. Play the clown; make your kids laugh at you, and encourage them to sing. They will feel more confident singing next to a dad who does not have a perfect voice.

Music is organized sounds that are structured using the four building blocks, namely, *melody, harmony*, *rhythm* and *dynamics*. Each of these four blocks triggers different responses within the body, with some crossovers. Music affects our body, mind, cognitive ability and behaviour in a very strong way.

Music has also been shown to have a direct influence on the heart rate. Depending on the tempo of the music, it can make us jump up and down quickly, or sway slowly.

Choosing good music to play in the house can go a long way in keeping a calm environment.

There can be different music for the morning and evening, and for special times when the whole family is together, and a good instrumental piece to play in the background during mealtimes, and so on. More than anything else, music can change or underpin our emotions. There are proven frequencies and harmonic sequences that trigger hormonal releases and affect our emotions.

Singing, even with broken notes and an ordinary or bad voice with kids during a pleasant activity like bathing, creates a very loving atmosphere.

###  94. One-Minute Magic

If you have only a few minutes with your kids, for example during a short drive and you want to make that connection really memorable, choose some uplifting music that will positively influence their state. Even just playing it in the background is sufficient to create the desired outcome. Make sure you choose music your kids find uplifting and do not make the choice based on your own preference. More often than not, the two are not the same.

###  95. One-Minute Magic

Sing before your children go to sleep. The song could be as basic as, 'You are the best, you are the best, and I love me and I love you.'

### Music and Intelligence

There are extensive research findings available that prove that music can have a positive impact on:

- Speech understanding
- Reading and spelling ability
- Behaviour
- Attention
- Concentration
- Academic achievement

(*See below for a graphical representation*)

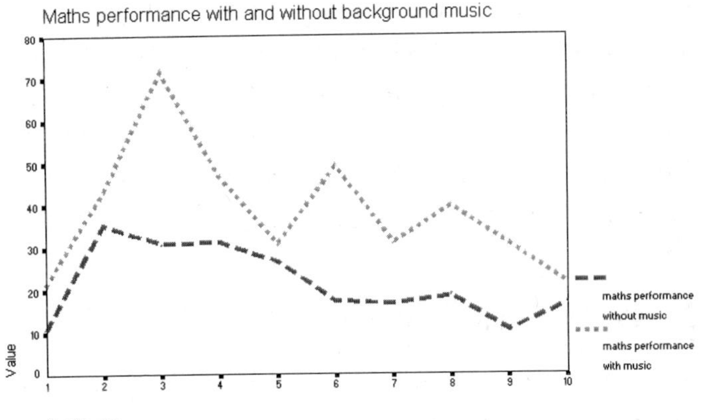


*Source:* 'Can listening to background music improve children's behaviour and performance in mathematics?' by Dr Susan Hallam and John Price, Institute of Education, University of London.

What happens is that the brain creates links between the music and the newly acquired knowledge. If later, the child is trying to remember what it learned, the brain follows the song it heard while learning and recalls the information faster. We can use this magical fact about our brain and create One-Minute Magic triggers!

### 96. One-Minute Magic

Every time you prepare breakfast, play a certain song. Your children will know subconsciously and consciously that food will be served soon. But on top of the conscious anticipation for food, the body will also react and get ready for food. It is magic! The kids often start coming to the dining table for the meal without any pestering. It sounds silly, but it works for many who have tried it.

### 97. One-Minute Magic

Choose a victory tune – a song that you play every time your child has done something great. The magic about this is, after a few dozen times, the brain associates the song with happiness. Because you played the song every time your child was happy, the brain linked happiness to this song. Guess what happens if you play the same song when your kid is unhappy. Exactly the same! Your brain says, 'Hey, this is the happy song' and it starts producing happy hormones. You will see your child light up! This is called 'anchoring' and is a powerful tool to quickly change emotions and influence behaviour as well as thoughts. All this is unfortunately not taught in any school or college curriculum.

###  98. One-Minute Magic

Choose a tune for each occasion, like sleeping, sports, etc. You can basically programme the brain with music. It is fascinating both for you and for others whom you spend time with. The amazing thing is, even though you *know* what is happening, it still works. And it gets even better. You do not need to play the actual song. You can hum it, whistle it, sing it or even use your hands to clap to the rhythm, and unless they are too far off to hear, their brain will know what you mean! Music is an incredible way to create triggers and if used correctly, it can be a wonderful tool in your quest to become a true super dad.

You can use this knowledge of 'settling down music' at home as well. Putting some music on takes less than a minute and it will make the experience so much more enjoyable for your whole family.

Try to get the kids to learn at least one musical instrument. It will serve them for life and you may discover a new talent in them.

### 99. One-Minute Magic

Ask your kids what their favourite music tunes are and keep a list to play when they are down or not feeling their best. As simple as it sounds, it inevitably works to some extent every time it is done.

# 10

# Blast-offs with Your Children: The Dos and Don'ts

Small things can make the biggest difference to our children. Whenever you need a quick super dad idea to have a great time with your kids, this chapter has everything you need. A quick blast-off may plant some good habit and mindset seeds too.

Note that most of these suggestions are not One-Minute Magic techniques, but they are blasts that you can have with your kids. If you can spare some extra time once in a while from your busy schedule, these work wonders.

Some of them will sound a bit silly and feel too childish, but then that is what childhood is all about. Raising kids, besides being a huge responsibility, is also an opportunity to have a second go at our own childhood and making up for many things that we missed out on decades ago. On many occasions, silly things are more fun for the kids and the bonding is more special during these activities, as the kids really feel that you are at their level and a friend for some time.

Here we go ...

**The Dos**

- Build an indoor tent using old sheets and chairs
- Teach them a tongue twister, like kachcha papad, pakka papad
- Play hide and seek
- Have a pillow fight
- Make a time capsule every few years to revisit in the future
- Go on a scavenger hunt
- Make paper airplanes
- Map out the family history with photos
- Fly a kite
- Create an obstacle course with chairs, boxes, bins, etc.
- Have a water fight

- Play shadow puppets
- Let your child decide what you are going to do that day – maybe a game of their choice
- Teach them how to skip stones across water
- Make a treasure hunt with maps and clues
- Make a shooting range with cans or paper cups. Use pea-shooters, nerve guns or tennis balls to knock them down
- Play hopscotch
- Go cloud-watching. Lie on the ground and look for shapes of animals or faces in the sky

- Write a short story together, draw some pictures and then staple it all together. You will be amazed how excited the kids are to see their names in a story
- Visit a museum or an art gallery
- Jump in some big puddles and relive your childhood with your kids
- Go bowling and don't mind slipping a few times
- Watch a movie together and try to make sure the kids indeed like it
- Find a hillock and roll down it (not if you have a back or joint problem)
- Visit an animal farm and feed some animals, or feed local birds and animals near your house
- Look out for shooting stars together and make a wish when you see one
- Write a love letter to each other – if you don't, the kids will write it anyway to you when they learn to write
- In summers, you can use socks rolled into a ball
- Play board games together
- Build models together, could use clay
- Do some house chores together
- Have plenty of tickle fights

- Just before bedtime, surprise them by taking them out for an ice cream in their pajamas. Just try to have a small interval before going to bed to avoid high blood sugar before sleeping. It's okay once in a while. Friday and Saturday nights work best for this
- Do some local volunteer work together such as helping in a community home or at an animal sanctuary
- Start a family blog that you all write
- Play detective by making a list of things around the home, like 'how many pictures are on the walls?' or 'how many objects use electricity?' and ask them to find the answers

- Do some random acts of kindness with your child. Give somebody some flowers, or write an anonymous note telling someone how lovely they are
- Plant a tree especially for them. Take annual pictures to see how much they grow

**Some more ideas**

- When with kids, answer a call saying, 'Hello! This is the proud father of ... (your kid's name)'
- Take silly photos of each other and create a laugh-out-loud album
- Plant something together, even if it is just a herb pot
- Track Santa on Christmas Eve. There are several websites with a 'Santa Tracker' that show where he is, en route to you
- Invent a cocktail by mixing different juices and food colourings. Do not forget to give it a special name – ideally it should have your kid's name
- List all the things that have changed since you were a child, reminding kids that you had wind-down car windows, rotary dial telephones, no remote control, etc. This cultivates gratitude

- Go swimming or to a water park. Water activities create good bonding
- Make a volcano from baking powder and vinegar
- Make a 'Love You' poster for their bedroom. Think of all the things you love about them and keep adding to it
- Go to a swap meet to buy or sell, or visit a garage sale. Can the kids bag a bargain? Don't wait till they grow up to teach them negotiation
- Make birthdays memorable. Try filling their bedroom with balloons while they are still asleep or put candles on every meal they eat that day
- Clean the house together
- Wash the dishes with them or let them place it in the dishwasher
- Set the dinner table together
- Watch educational TV channels and discuss the topics raised
- Mow the lawn together
- Plan a family talent show. Stage a play in the living room, a real simple one. Kids would want their turn first and just cannot wait to act if encouraged well
- Call up grandparents together, if they live elsewhere

- Solve brain-teasers
- Build a tree house
- Memorize some important phone numbers. This is an important skill in the modern day, as very often a person does not remember his own telephone number due to the features in modern phones and gadgets. Memory is a muscle in the brain, which can be made stronger by using it
- Count the calories of a meal together
- Act out a story and let others guess it
- Sketch as you go on a nature trail
- Carve soap animals
- Play with clay

The activities mentioned above may look silly or too ordinary. But they have been carefully selected and are time-tested. They definitely impact the kids' minds, beliefs and habits for a lifetime.

### The Don'ts

Don't ever do these in front of your kids:

- Say, 'I give up'
- Watch violent movies
- Shout at or criticize your wife

- Watch sex scenes
- Swear
- Email or text, especially when your children are talking to you
- Play violent video games
- Make racial or sexist remarks
- Criticize your children
- Criticize your wife
- Rely on junk food
- Speak badly of others
- Act bored when your children want to share something with you
- Throw litter on the road
- Be rude to waiters or service personnel

**Never Ever:**

- Say, 'because I said so' to a why/why not question
- Refuse to help your children without full reasons when they ask
- Favour one child over another
- Overprotect your children
- Hit your children
- Compare your child with another
- Belittle your child, especially in front of another person
- Gamble/bet in front of them

- Criticize their school work without explaining why
- Say that you are too tired to read a bedtime story. Would you miss a call from the office for the same reason? Find a way to do whatever you feel is really important unless you think your work is more important than your child
- Tell them 'you are being oversensitive and are overreacting' on an issue
- Moan about missing something (a TV show, etc.) because of them
- Let them do things their mom would not let them do
- Say yes when your wife says no
- Scratch or fiddle with your groin in front of them
- Play music with offensive lyrics in the car or at home
- Tell them life was better when they were smaller
- Ask them to fetch your cigarettes, lighter, or beer cans
- Giggle when a toddler says their first swear word
- Get mad when your child embarrasses you in public
- Criticize a dish they have made for you

- Use your kids to spy on people for you
- Push your child to like something just because you do
- Forget to say 'I love you' every day
- Make your child feel too guilty for something they have done
- Steal their candy
- Discriminate between a son and a daughter
- Argue with your wife and stomp out of the house
- Leave the toilet seat up or a gate open
- Ignore your Father's Day present and not give a return gift
- Call your kid fat or big
- Confront your child when they are upset
- Do your own things instead of giving priority to your kids' needs

# 11
# Some True Magic Moment Stories of Dads

While writing this book, I reached out to dads across the world to hear their own 'magic moment' stories. I received hundreds of them. Here are some of my favourite, heart-warming magic moments, which were sent by dads from around the world. Most of them are written in first person.

### Do I know you?

I was working overseas during the first six years of my son's life. Due to this, his mother and my parents raised him (we are a joint family). When my job contract ended, I returned to my country and everyone at home came to the airport to welcome me back.

When my son saw me at the airport, he ran to me and gave me the biggest hug I have ever received and said, 'I do not remember you, but I missed you very much.'

I actually cried in public.

### Oh, Dad

One day I took my eleven-year-old daughter to a small park. I spotted a pond, which had some boats for *'pay and use'* and thought it would be fun to go sailing together, even though I did not really know how to work a sailboat.

We got off to a good start, but when the breeze got strong, our little boat started going in circles and tipped over, landing us in a few feet of water. We had to be helped back to shore.

'I am sorry, Sally,' I said sadly.

Trying to cheer me up, she said, 'Dad, *anyone* can go on a boat and *sail* a mile or two, but how many people can say that their boat *sank?* Not many!'

### Sorry, God

It is our family tradition to stand before God for a minute before leaving our home. Once, I was so engrossed in an office call that I picked up my laptop bag and rushed through the door towards my car.

My three-year-old daughter went to our prayer room and said, 'Sorry, God! Dad forgot to say bye to you. But do not worry; he will come home early today!'

## First steps

I watched in awe the first time my son sat up and smiled, but my very favourite memory is when he took his first steps. With unsteady legs and his arms out like Frankenstein's, he waddled towards me. When he got to me, he threw his arms around and gave me a slobbery kiss.

I am so grateful I was there and did not miss that out!

## My little Superman

One day, my son was being Superman and decided to 'fly' over the ditch I was digging in the garden. He did not quite make the leap of faith and fell into the shallow ditch. When I lifted him out, he proudly exclaimed, 'Dad, I would have made it with a cape!'

## Daddy, Daddy

My son just started Little League and although he tries, he can't hit the ball. One evening, my son had a formal game and I could not attend it, as I had to work late. So I told him that I wanted to hear all about the game when I got back home.

Afterwards, he ran into the house yelling, 'Daddy! Daddy! I got three hits today!' He pointed to his shoulder, his arm and his foot and exclaimed, 'Here, here and here!'

### On your side

My son and I were canoeing. Well, whenever I moved my paddle from one side of the canoe to the other, my son moved his too – we were just going in circles. When I asked him, he said, 'Dad, we are on the same team. If we are on the same team, we have to be on the same side.' We kept paddling. We did not get very far but we went miles in our relationship.

### Sorry, too busy!

I could not stop laughing when I called my four-year-old daughter for dinner. She was playing with her toy and replied, 'I am typing an important mail, you start and I will join you in a few minutes.'

### Will you marry me?

My three-year-old daughter and I were watching television when I felt the urge to hug her and tell her I love her. Pulling her toward me, I squeezed her and said, 'I love you.'

She replied, 'I love you too.'

'I love you three,' I smiled.

She astonished me by saying, 'Will you marry me?'

### It's more than a wall

I was tending to our three-year-old daughter. After a few minutes, I realized the house was quiet, too quiet. I figured it was time to find Kapri and see what she was doing. Just then, she came running to me, shouting, 'Daddy, come see my *bootiful drawing*.'

Uh oh!

She led me to the front door and proudly pointed to the colourful scribbles on the wall. Made with a permanent marker! She was so proud of her artwork that I paused to ask myself, 'What is more important – the wall or my daughter?' and replied, 'Oh what a beautiful drawing. Let us frame it.'

We had fun making a wooden photo frame to fit over her 'artwork' and now when people visit, they too can enjoy Kapri's artistic impression.

### What really matters?

I bought some nice speakers for my stereo system. One day, my five-year-old son was wrestling with a friend and made a hole in one of the speakers by accident. Trembling, he came to me to narrate what had happened. I saw his face and knew the last thing he needed was a scolding. He was already scared enough.

I placed my hands on his quivering shoulders and said, 'You are more important than the speakers. I can replace the speaker, but I cannot replace you.' I will never forget the look on his face when he realized that.

### Night-night Daddy

One night, I was too sick to tuck my two-year-old in bed, so she came to my bedroom. She tucked me in, saying, 'Daddy, *seep* tight, do not let *da* bed bugs bite. *I wuv you.*'

### Bad timing!

I was scheduled to speak at a conference. On my way out, my nine-month-old daughter reached out for me, so I lovingly picked her up and you guessed it – she peed on me! I was soaked.

At the conference, at the start of my presentation, I told the audience what had happened with me earlier in the day, as I just could not resist telling it. They loved it – at least they did not have to sit through another boring presentation! I received more appreciation for this talk than I ever had for any of my presentations before. They probably had kids too.

### Do not stop me now

One day, my son was dipping his fingers in the peanut butter jar. With peanut butter all over his mouth and hands, he looked up to see my look of horror. Wide-eyed and innocent, he grinned and asked, 'Do you still love me, Daddy?'

I laughed and said, 'I will always love you.' He smiled and carried on eating.

### Sorry

I was in a horrible mood when I left work and had to pick up the kids. On the drive home, the kids started hitting each other in the back seat. After asking them to stop several times, I snapped and said, 'If you do not stop right now, I am pulling the car over and you can both get out!' I felt horrible afterwards, but it worked and they fell silent.

When we arrived home, I turned to them and said, 'I am sorry I yelled at you. It has been a really bad day and you were not listening to me. Sometimes even grown-ups react without thinking first.' The kids replied, 'No Daddy! You at least spoke to us.' I really felt like garbage.

### Please Dad!

One day, my son Tim and I were walking in a poor neighbourhood when we spotted a homeless man sitting by a wooden crate. He was not begging, but his face was sad and worn. Tim had never encountered a homeless man before and asked him what was wrong. The man said, 'My dog just died. It was the only thing that made my life worthwhile.' Tim looked up with pleading eyes and asked, 'Can we get him a dog?'

We took the man to a nearby animal shelter where he picked out a dog. We paid for the dog's licence and gave it to the grateful stranger. Later that day, I bought Tim a toy he had been wanting for some time. When I gave it to him, I asked, 'What was better? Getting the slingshot or helping the homeless man?' Tim answered, 'I am happy to get this toy, but it was much more fun to see how happy we made that man.'

### Don't worry, be happy

When I arrived home from work after a stressful day, my four-year-old ran to me and hugged my leg. I told her to sit down and stop jumping around. She noticed my mood and quietly asked, 'What happened, Papa? Did your teacher ask you to leave class today? Don't worry, tomorrow you go to her and say you're sorry and she'll be happy.'

Finally, I had a smile on my face and said, 'Okay, I'll do that. Thank you.'

# Afterword

And so here you have it, the *One-Minute Super Dad* handbook. I hope you have enjoyed reading it as much as I have enjoyed writing it. Reach for it whenever you need a helping hand. It only takes a minute for many things to make a difference. This book is a friend by your side.

Have a joyous, meaningful and fulfilling time with your kids and please do not forget to have lots of fun.

**Dr Prashant Jindal**
**December 2017**

# Acknowledgements

I am very grateful to my parents whose unconditional love is the fuel of my life. While writing this book, I had flashbacks of many wonderful incidents that were long forgotten.

Thanks to my wife Deepti, my children Prisha and Krish, my brother Pawan, my mom and my aunt Oji for their love and support.

I am deeply indebted to my dear friends mentioned below (not in any particular order) for making this project possible:

- Raymond Aaron, co-author of the phenomenal *Chicken Soup for the Parent's Soul*
- Dr John Gray, author of *Men Are from Mars, Women Are from Venus and Children Are from Heaven*
- Sharon Lechter, co-author of *Rich Dad, Poor Dad* and former adviser of President George Bush's counsel on financial literacy

- Jay Niblick, author of *What's Your Genius?*
- Stephanie Hale, author of *Millionaire Women, Millionaire You*
- Tony Robbins, for being such an inspirational friend
- Ramesh Mittal, a great guide
- Craig Richards, noted musician
- Alison Turriff, noted composer
- Gary King, celebrity speaker
- Murielle Maupoint, Live-it Publications
- Siddhesh Inamdar, my obsessively perfectionist editor
- Krishan Chopra, Publisher, HarperCollins India, for his valuable insights and support in completing the book
- And, finally, special thanks to Ananth Padmanabhan, for his passionate involvement in publishing the book at HarperCollins